Proclaiming Grace & Freedom

The Story of United Methodism in America

John G. McEllhenney, editor
Frederick E. Maser
Kenneth E. Rowe
Charles Yrigoyen, Jr.

ABINGDON PRESS
Nashville

Book design by Blair Simon
Illustrations by Ann Simon
Typography by Simon Communications

Proclaiming Grace & Freedom: The Story of United Methodism in America
Copyright © 1982 by Abingdon Press. Illustrations © 1982 by Simon Communications.

Library of Congress Cataloging in Publication Data

Proclaiming grace and freedom.

    1. United Methodist Church (U.S.)—History.   2. Methodist Church—
United States—History.   I. McEllhenney, John G.

BX832.2A4P76   1982   287'.673   82-8800   AACR2

ISBN 0-687-34323-2

The poem "Outwitted" by Edwin Markham is used by permission of The
Markham Archives, Hormann Library of Wagner College.

Manufactured by the Parthenon Press at
Nashville, Tennessee, United States of America

Preface

The Ardmore, Pennsylvania, United Methodist Church has a heritage of helping people understand Methodism. During the period when Clinton M. Cherry was the church's pastor, he wrote *The Beliefs of a Methodist Christian*, a book many readers have found invaluable. Now the church presents *Proclaiming Grace and Freedom: The Story of United Methodism in America* as a bicentennial gift to American Methodism.

In the spring of 1979, the Ardmore church invited Frederick E. Maser, former executive secretary of the World Methodist Historical Society; Charles Yrigoyen, Jr., then a professor at Albright College in Reading, Pennsylvania, and now the general secretary of the General Commission on Archives and History of The United Methodist Church; and Kenneth E. Rowe, a professor and Methodist librarian at Drew University in Madison, New Jersey, to give a series of Lenten lectures on the history of United Methodism in America. From their lectures came the idea for this book.

Ardmore church's participation did not end with conceiving the idea of this book, however. The pastor became its editor. Blair Simon, who chairs the church's administrative council, is its designer and typographer. Another member, artist Ann Simon, drew the illustrations. Margaret W. Braun, church secretary extraordinary, typed the manuscript.

The writers of *Proclaiming Grace and Freedom* think it will serve several purposes. Each is highlighted by the way the book is indexed.

First, the book tells the story of United Methodism in America. Names of the principal actors in this drama are found in the Index, as are references to key events.

Second, the story of United Methodism is a tale of churches forming, separating, and coming together again. Accounts of these churches are woven into the narrative, but it is possible to isolate each church's own history by checking its entry in the Index.

Third, six characteristics of a complete church are listed on pages 2-3 of the Introduction. Every Index entry that pertains to one of these characteristics has the word *characteristic* in parentheses and a number from one to six, referring to the number of a characteristic described in the Introduction. By pursuing these listings, the reader will be able to judge how adequately United Methodism has embodied the characteristics of a complete church.

The result of this way of organizing the Index is that individuals and groups have three ways of reading *Proclaiming Grace and Freedom:* as a straightforward report on more than two hundred years of United Methodism in America; as separate stories of the churches that now compose The United Methodist Church; and as an essay on the characteristics of a complete church.

And now to the book itself, whose chronology is unfolded in the Contents by means of a time-line that lists key United Methodist happenings side by side with secular events.

John G. McEllhenney
Pastor, Ardmore United Methodist Church

The Eighteenth Century

1732   Georgia Colony founded

1772   *English court rules that a slave is free on landing in England*

1783   *Britain recognizes United States Independence*

1800   *Thomas Jefferson elected President of the United States*

1812   *Congress declares war on Great Britain*

Contents

Introduction by John G. McEllhenney *1*
Part One by Frederick E. Maser

I. **Beginnings in America** *9*   1735
   The Mission to Georgia and Beyond *9*
   The Soil for Planting *12*
   The Origins of the Church of the
   United Brethren in Christ *13*
       Philip William Otterbein *13*
       Martin Boehm *14*
   The Origins of Organized American Methodism *15*
       The Lay Immigrants *15*
       The First Preachers—Boardman and Pilmore *18*
       Reenforcements—Asbury and Wright *19*
       Pilmore's Southern Journey and Its Importance *20*

II. **Events Leading to a New Church** *21*   1773
   The First Conference of American Methodist Preachers *21*
   Political Crisis—The Revolutionary War *23*
   Spiritual Crisis—The Sacramental Controversy *24*
   Wesley's Plan for American Methodism *26*
   The Christmas Conference—1784 *28*

III. **The Churches of United Methodism and**   1784
   Their Early Progress *33*
   The Evangelical Association *33*
       Jacob Albright *33*
       Growth and Development *34*
   The Church of the United Brethren in Christ *36*
       Organization *36*
       Expansion *36*
   Some Characteristics of the Churches *37*
       Doctrines and Practices *37*
       Splits and Schisms *39*
       The Churches Take Shape *42*
       Camp Meetings and Revivalism *44*
       Last Days of Otterbein, Boehm, and Asbury *44*   1816

The Nineteenth Century

1815 | *Napoleon is defeated at the Battle of Waterloo*

1844 | *Samuel Morse sends the first telegraph message, "What hath God wrought!"*

1863 | *President Lincoln issues the Emancipation Proclamation*

1903 | *Wright brothers launch the first successful manned flight*

1905 | *Albert Einstein proposes the theory of relativity*

Contents

Part Two by Charles Yrigoyen, Jr.

I. **Growth and Development** *49*   **1816**
    The Second Great Awakening and Social Reform *50*
    Keys to Continued Growth *51*
        Dedication *52*
        Organization *53*
        Language Restrictions *54*
    Worship, Education, Missions, and Publication *55*
        Worship *55*
        Education *56*
        Missions *59*
        Publication *60*
    Democratic Crises and the
    Methodist Protestant Church *61*

II. **Slavery, Division, and Civil War** *63*   **1844**
    Methodists and Abolition *64*
    The General Conference of 1844 *65*
    Formation of the Methodist
    Episcopal Church, South *67*
    Northern and Southern
    Methodists Go Their Own Ways *68*
    Lincoln's Election and Civil War *70*

III. **New Challenges** *73*   **1866**
    The Nation Begins to Change *73*
    The Churches Prosper *75*
    Publishing, Education, and Worship *75*
    Theological and Structural Controversies *77*
    Lay Participation *79*
    Missionary Work *82*
    Social Problems *84*
    Interchurch Cooperation *86*
    Whither? *87*   **1913**

Introduction

by John G. McEllhenney

United Methodist history is closely related to happenings outside the church. Nowhere is this relationship clearer than in May 1738, the month often singled out as containing the event that launched Methodism. On May 12, Samuel Johnson—a Christian moralist and author of the classic English Dictionary—published a satirical poem in which he claimed that rich Londoners were cold-hearted in their treatment of the poor. On the 24th, John Wesley—the father of Methodism—went to a prayer meeting in London and became warm-hearted in his preaching of the gospel to rich and poor alike.

It may be coincidental that these things happened in the same month, or they may have been woven together by God to show that the gospel was not reaching the people who needed to hear it—the rich who were doing nothing about the plight of the poor, and the poor who were so despairing that they used the few pennies they had to drown their anguish in gin.

Both Wesley and Johnson were members of the Church of England—a church that preserved Christ's barbed words for those who thought themselves to be physically, morally, or spiritually rich; a church that also preserved Christ's hopeful words for those who knew themselves to be physically, morally, or spiritually poor. But the barbed message was not getting at the smug people dozing in Church of England pews, and the comforting message was not getting out of church to people scrambling for crumbs of bread and hope.

Although Wesley and Johnson were in no sense collaborators, they found ways to get their church's message to the people who needed to hear it. Johnson, a layman, wrote poems and essays in which he called rich Londoners back to moral living. Wesley, a priest, began to preach in such a way that those who knew they needed God heard him gladly.

The essence of United Methodism is found in the design that wove together in May 1738, Johnson's word of reproach for those who considered themselves irreproachable and Wesley's word of hope for those who were hopeless. United Methodism links laity and clergy in a ministry of proclaiming that God was in Christ bringing salvation to the world. And it links mind and heart in keeping that message true to the fullness of the biblical revelation and personal for each believer.

United Methodism believes that only by being a complete church can it preserve the fullness of the biblical revelation and assist individuals in finding a personal faith. It draws its understanding of completeness from three of the principal communions of the Protestant Reformation: the Church of England, through John Wesley; the Lutheran Church, through Jacob Albright; and the Reformed Church, through Philip William Otterbein. Each of these churches used the Bible, Christian tradition, careful thinking, and accumulated practical experience to define the characteristics of a complete church:

1. A complete church orders worship, preaching, hymnody, prayer, and the sacraments in such manner that the fullness of the biblical revelation and the various moods of believers are expressed in language of poetic power.

2. A complete church has a heritage of thinking about the Christian faith and applying it to daily living that is steeped in the Bible and flavored by insights drawn from literature, history, philosophy, and the natural and social sciences.

3. A complete church devises a system of church government that takes sin seriously and therefore does not lodge power in one group of persons without lodging balancing power in another group.

4. A complete church provides Christian education for young and old alike, often using Sunday schools, and gives a systematic theological education to persons preparing for the ordained ministry.

5. A complete church develops such institutions as mission boards and agencies of moral reform, colleges and publishing houses, hospitals and orphanages, in response to Jesus' teachings.

6. A complete church uses the best that humans can produce—architecture, music, sculpture, poetry, painting, and fiction—in the service of God.

Churches are complete when these six characteristics are present. Parts 2 and 3 of this book describe United Methodism's efforts to achieve completeness by showing a concern for church constitutions, worship, education, missions, theology, social outreach, and publishing. But United Methodist history begins in part 1, where the spiritual chilliness of some complete churches is described and where the stories are told of organized Methodism coming to America and of the development of the United Brethren and Evangelical movements.

The churches that now compose The United Methodist Church were born in the eighteenth century, during a time when a number of Christian denominations were using their best thinkers to fashion a message true to the fullness of the biblical revelation. That message was not warming hearts, however, because church leaders were indifferent to its communication. They did not help individuals find within the system of carefully thought out Christian beliefs a set of heartfelt personal convictions.

Such indifference to the communication of the gospel did not go unchallenged. Persons were gathering all over northern Europe and the American colonies for the purpose of finding a warm personal faith and the courage to make life better for society's outcasts. London in 1738 had at least thirty groups of religious seekers. Their leaders struck sparks that ignited in persons a desire to accept for themselves God's offer of forgiveness and new life in Christ.

Leaders of these renewal groups, as we might call them, were for the most part committed to the complete churches in which they first learned about Christianity. Although they found these churches spiritually cool, they wanted to remain within them and blow on their dying coals of spirituality. But the churches were suspicious of these heralds of hearty Christian faith. How could they be sure the reformers were not really revolutionaries who were intent, not on rekindling fires, but on destroying the fireplaces? Because of this uncertainty, renewal leaders often found themselves unwelcome in the established churches.

Part 1 of this book is the story of renewal movements — the Methodist within the Church of England, the United Brethren within the Reformed Church, and the Evangelical within the Lutheran Church — that failed to find a welcome in the churches of their day and therefore formed their own. As they made the shift from renewal group to church, their principal concern was: How much of the old do you hang onto?

Some religious revolutionaries wanted to throw the Christian past into a bonfire, in the hope that after the holocaust was over, a few things would be found among the ashes that really deserved to endure. For them, nothing from the past was needed to give God something to work with in the present—not forms of worship, written sermons, prayer books, the sacraments, volumes of theology and ethics, church constitutions, and educated clergy. For a few, not even Bibles were deemed necessary. These spiritual revolutionaries wanted to blow the Christian past to smithereens so that God could begin afresh.

Opposing the revolutionaries were religious reformers who believed that God always works with the old in creating the new and that therefore the past must be preserved. They recognized that they owed the basis for their new birth in Christ to churches that were embodying the six characteristics of completeness. They understood that hearts are not automatically warmed where forms of worship, the sacraments, and ordained clergy are present. But they also understood that only where basic Christian teachings are preserved is God able to warm individual hearts. Therefore, conservative religious reformers moved quickly to draft church constitutions that would provide, however tentatively in some cases, for ordered worship, Christian education, church government, theological instruction, and a variety of benevolent institutions.

The founders of United Methodism were conservative reformers. They saved much of the past as they organized new churches in which persons heard the old story of Jesus told in such a way that their hearts were warmed and their minds enriched. In the following pages the reader will watch what has just been described slowly unfolding in history.

Part One

The Eighteenth Century

by Frederick E. Maser

The first attempt at something like Methodism to America, the mission of John and Charles Wesley to the Native Americans of Georgia, was a comparative failure. The brothers left England for James Oglethorpe's Georgia colony in 1735 — John as a pastor to the colonists and missionary to the Indians, Charles as the governor's secretary. When they returned home less than two years later, they were not sure they had preached the gospel efficaciously; they were not even certain of their own faith in Christ.

I. Beginnings in America—
1735 to 1773

Many United Methodists are unaware that the early leaders of their denomination were members of a variety of churches. John and Charles Wesley were lifelong priests in the Church of England; Philip William Otterbein never resigned from the German Reformed Church; Martin Boehm belonged to a Mennonite church from which he was later expelled; and Jacob Albright was a Lutheran. In addition some are unaware that their denomination was, partially at least, the outgrowth of a succession of missions to America, the first of which was a comparative failure.

The Mission to Georgia and Beyond

John and Charles Wesley, priests of the Church of England, which is also called the Anglican Church, embarked for Georgia in 1735 as missionaries to the Indians and to care for the spiritual welfare of the colonists. They came from Oxford University where they had formed small groups of students who regularly attended Holy Communion and gathered for daily prayer, fasting, frequent self-examination, and Bible study. Later they began to aid the poor and the imprisoned and to assist in tutoring their children. The strict rules they laid down to govern themselves led other students to term them "Methodists."

On coming to Georgia the Wesleys tried to force this

rigid Methodism on the colonists without much success. John worked with the children, published his first hymnal, and faithfully fulfilled his duties as a pastor. However, the inflexible manner in which the brothers carried out their religious practices soon alienated the majority of the colonists except for the Moravian settlers and a small group of serious-minded people whom John formed into a Methodist class. The Moravians, some of whom the brothers had met on their voyage to Georgia, emphasized life in the spirit, evangelization, and mission. They stressed faith in Christ in terms of personal trust, commitment, and love rather than in terms of duty. The brothers often attended their services.

The mission of the Wesleys to the Indians was also unsuccessful, and in 1736 Charles returned home. John became involved in a scandal when he refused Holy Communion to Sophey Hopkey, niece of the chief magistrate of Savannah, because she failed to follow certain church rules. Wesley was arrested and indicted on numerous charges, the most serious of which was the defamation of Sophey's character. Though he repeatedly sought action from the courts, he was never brought to trial. When he fled the colony in 1737, the first stage of Methodism in America was ended.

In the meantime, George Whitefield, an Anglican priest and also a member of the Oxford Methodists, came to the new world and served in Georgia for a time as the successor to John Wesley. He later became one of the outstanding leaders of the Great Awakening—a revival movement that began in the middle colonies, thrived in New England under the preaching of Jonathan Edwards, then died down, only to be revived by Whitefield and others between 1739 and 1742. Whitefield went back and forth between England and America thirteen times, preaching wherever he went.

The Wesleys, back in England, had met some Moravians through whom they were led to a personal experience of faith in Christ accompanied by an assurance of salvation. Both the brothers enjoyed this deepening of their religious faith at about the same time. John's experience took place at a Moravian prayer meeting in London's Aldersgate Street on May 24, 1738. It is better known than that of his brother because of the oft-quoted line from his *Journal*, "I felt my heart strangely warmed."

The effect on the Wesleys was little short of miraculous. They began to preach with new confidence, power, and love. In addition, they continued their Oxford custom of forming their converts into small groups.

John Wesley's message centered in a handful of simple truths: because of sin, persons need to be saved; by faith in the redemptive work of Christ, they can be saved; through faith in Christ, they can receive the assurance of their salvation; and through the Holy Spirit they can receive the gift of Christian perfection, either instantly or by spiritual development. The change in the believer wrought by faith in Christ is referred to as the new birth. The fruit of the experience is a new life expressed in daily Christian conduct. And the believer was expected to use the means of grace, namely, church attendance, prayer, Bible study, participation in the Holy Communion, and fasting.

The new movement spread, and soon England was dotted with Methodist societies. When additional preachers were needed Wesley, encouraged by his mother, began to select gifted lay persons to preach in the societies, many of which had erected their own buildings. However, Wesley made it exceedingly clear that the movement was not a new church, but rather a renewal movement within the Church of England. Methodists went to Anglican priests to receive the sacraments, and they conducted no meetings of their own when services were being held in the local parish church.

While Wesley's work was expanding in England, Whitefield continued to preach in America, but he never formed in America the societies of devout Christians that characterized Wesley's work in England. His chief importance for Methodism lay in the fact that he prepared the ground for later Methodist work. Before continuing our story, however, it might be well to discover what America was like in the days of Whitefield and Wesley.

The Soil for Planting

By the middle of the eighteenth century the American colonies were populated by a growing, bustling, independent people. The immigrants were mostly from northern Europe and Great Britain; and by 1760 Anglicans, Baptists, Congregationalists, Dutch and German Reformed, Jews, Lutherans, Moravians, Presbyterians, Quakers, Roman Catholics, and a handful of small sects were on the scene. In certain colonies some denominations had succeeded in becoming the established religion, that is, the religion supported by the state. No one denomination, however, had been able to capture the entire seaboard. Diversity marked the social and religious backgrounds of the colonists. Probably all classes of British and European life, except royalty, were represented.

The population of the colonies grew rapidly. In 1650 the population was 52,000. In 1700 it had grown to 250,000, and by 1760 to 1,700,000. In 1770 there were about two million persons in the colonies, in 1780 nearer three million, and by 1790 almost four million. These persons had been uprooted from familiar surroundings and thrust into a new situation where they experienced that lost feeling so often the result of change. They needed the help and direction that religion can give.

In contrast to Europe and England, there was a spirit of democracy abroad in the colonies. This spirit was partly due to the Great Awakening, which had proclaimed that *all* persons are sinners in need of a Savior. It was furthered by the circumstances of colonial life. The family into which one was born was an important factor in deciding one's place in the old world, but it had less importance in the colonies where skill, flexibility, inventiveness, adaptability, and the willingness to work hard carried more weight than a person's coat of arms.

In spite of all these factors, which offered a rare opportunity for Methodism, John Wesley did not seek to evangelize the new world at this time, and George Whitefield failed to organize Methodist-type societies in America. However, in 1752 Philip William Otterbein came to America. He was a preacher destined to evangelize large numbers of Germans here and, later, to join forces with Martin Boehm, leader of the Boehm revival. Eventually, the two men would organize the Church of the United Brethren in Christ.

The Origins of the Church of the United Brethren in Christ

Philip William Otterbein

Philip William Otterbein was born in Germany June 3, 1726. His father, uncle, and five brothers were all ministers in the German Reformed Church, and his sister married a minister. He received the equivalent of a university education and was nurtured in a mellowed Calvinism. He was ordained in 1749 and became pastor of a German Reformed church. Because his forthright sermons disturbed his people, they were probably glad when he answered a call to serve German Reformed people in the new world.

Otterbein arrived in America July 28, 1752, and became pastor of a German Reformed congregation in Lancaster, Pennsylvania, the second largest German Reformed church in America. Here he learned that forthright preaching does not necessarily meet everyone's religious needs. In 1754, after preaching a stirring sermon on God's grace, Otterbein was confronted by a man, convinced of his own sinfulness, who asked about the meaning of grace. Otterbein shook his head and said sadly, "Advice is scarce with me this day." Otterbein went into his study, locked the door, and resolved never to preach again until he had obtained the peace and joy of a conscious salvation. Through a religious experience not unlike that of John Wesley, he became convinced of the reality of divine forgiveness and the assurance of salvation. He began to preach with a new fervor, not only in his own church, but also in southeastern Pennsylvania and Maryland. In 1767 he met Martin Boehm, the man with whom he became the co-founder of the Church of the United Brethren in Christ.

Martin Boehm

Boehm, of Swiss extraction, was born in Lancaster County, Pennsylvania, in 1725. He and his family were staunch Mennonites who traced their spiritual lineage to the sixteenth-century reformer, Menno Simons. In the eighteenth century many of his followers came to America and settled in Maryland, Virginia, and Pennsylvania. They accepted the Protestant emphasis on the Bible, but they rejected formal church organization and infant baptism. It was their custom to select their pastors by lot, and Boehm was chosen in 1758. He was naturally shy and found it difficult to preach. His sense of inadequacy drove him to a deeper prayer life and to Bible study through which he experienced forgiveness and received an assurance of salvation and Christ's presence.

Like Otterbein, Boehm began to preach in surrounding German communities, and in 1767 he announced a "big meeting" in Isaac Long's barn, six miles northeast of Lancaster. Otterbein, hearing of the gathering, entered the barn while Boehm was preaching. When the service was ended, he made his way to Boehm, clasped him in his powerful arms and said, *Wir sind Brüder!* ("We are brothers!") Otterbein and Boehm joined forces in preaching evangelical doctrines among the German-speaking people. They enlisted other preachers and formed a fellowship based, not upon organization, but upon similarity of religious experience. By 1773 they had formed societies in Pennsylvania, Virginia, and Maryland.

The Origins of Organized American Methodism

The Lay Immigrants

Organized Methodism in America began as a lay movement. Whereas Whitefield and the Wesleys failed to establish permanent Methodist societies in the new world, three laymen secured a firm foothold for Methodist societies in the colonies. Robert Strawbridge, an immigrant farmer, organized Methodism in Maryland around 1760 or shortly thereafter; Philip Embury, an immigrant carpenter and teacher, began work in New York City in 1766; and in 1767 Captain Thomas Webb, a retired soldier of the British army, formed Methodist societies in Philadelphia and other places. By 1766 Methodism had also begun in Leesburg, Virginia, possibly through the work of Strawbridge and others, and by 1768 a building had been erected there for Methodist use.

These early meetinghouses were usually very plain square or rectangular structures. They were either of log, brick, or stone, and not all of them had windows. Those built in urban centers contained windows and a pulpit. In some a balcony was an added feature.

Strawbridge, who formed the first Methodist society on

the Wesleyan plan in America, had come from Ireland around 1760 and had settled in Frederick County, Maryland. Having preached as a Methodist in Ireland, he not only continued his practice of preaching in the new world but also built a log meetinghouse about a mile from his home — the first Methodist meetinghouse in America. He traveled throughout the eastern shore of Maryland, Virginia, and other places organizing Methodist societies, and was especially useful in challenging young men to become preachers.

Philip Embury also came from Ireland. He had been converted under Wesley from whom he received a license to preach. In 1760 Embury, his wife, and two or three of his brothers, together with Paul and Barbara Heck, sailed for America. It was not until 1766, however, that he began preaching because of the prodding of Barbara Heck, who helped him gather his first congregation of five persons. The first meeting was held in Embury's house, but on October 30, 1768, the group, which had grown in numbers, dedicated a small meetinghouse in John Street, New York.

Captain Thomas Webb organized the Methodists in Philadelphia. He had been converted in England, joining a Methodist society in Bristol in 1765. Wesley used him as a preacher in and about Bristol and Bath. The Captain always wore a green patch over his right eye, having lost his eye in a battle in Quebec Province. Webb eventually returned to America as barrack master at Albany, a position amounting to retirement. Hearing of the work of Embury in New York, he assisted him by preaching and later by contributing money to the building of John Street meetinghouse. In 1767 he made his way to Philadelphia where he found a small group of persons meeting in a sail loft. Two of them had been converted by Whitefield. He organized the group into The Religious Society of Protestants called Methodists.

*E*arly *United Brethren, Evangelical, and Methodist preachers—frequently they were not ordained—spoke to people wherever they found them: on the docks, in fields, private homes, playhouses, courthouses, and taverns. But as soon as they made converts, they brought them together for Bible study, prayer, mutual admonition, and love feasts. It was not long, therefore, before church buildings were needed.*

The First Preachers—Boardman and Pilmore

As the work grew in Maryland, New York, Philadelphia, and Virginia, some of Strawbridge's converts in Maryland, and Thomas Taylor, a trustee of the society in New York, wrote to John Wesley urging him to send preachers to the new world. Wesley asked for volunteers, and Richard Boardman and Joseph Pilmore offered themselves for service in America. They arrived in Philadelphia late in October 1769. The men had known only of the work in New York and Maryland and were surprised to discover that Captain Webb was in Philadelphia and had formed a Methodist society now numbering about one hundred people. Pilmore remained in Philadelphia to minister to this group, and Boardman, who had been designated by Wesley as his chief assistant in America, went to New York. The men exchanged places frequently.

Pilmore set about securing a new building for the growing Philadelphia society. After searching for a suitable meetinghouse without success, they finally purchased a huge shell of a building from a man whose son—described by Pilmore as *non compos mentis*—had purchased it at auction. It belonged originally to a splinter group from a German Reformed church and was called St. George's. The interior of the church was not completed, however, until after the Revolutionary War.

The Methodists moved into the bare building on November 24, 1769, and on December 3 Pilmore made an important statement of the faith and practices of the Methodists to a large gathering. He pointed out that the Methodist movement had never been designed to make a separation from the Church of England. He also stated that Methodism was intended for the benefit of all those in every denomination who "earnestly desire to flee from the wrath to come."

A person could thus be a Methodist and retain membership in his or her own church. The Methodists, he explained, had come to revive spiritual religion, to proclaim that Christ died for us in order to live in us and reign over us in all things.

Reenforcements — Asbury and Wright

The response to the leadership of both Pilmore and Boardman was immediate, and in 1770 Pilmore wrote to Wesley in most enthusiastic terms about conditions in America, stating that there was work enough for at least two more preachers.

At first there was no disposition on the part of the British preachers to come to America. Wesley, himself, thought for a time of returning to the colonies, but in 1771 five preachers volunteered for work in the new world. The two chosen by Wesley were Richard Wright and Francis Asbury. Wright was never very successful in the American work, but the choice of twenty-six-year-old Francis Asbury proved a wise one. He was a dedicated preacher with a firm grasp of Methodist principles and discipline. He was a born leader, and although he was not appointed as Wesley's assistant in America to succeed Richard Boardman until October 1772, he nevertheless took charge at once. He enforced Methodist discipline and expressed dissatisfaction with the work of Pilmore and Boardman because it was confined too greatly to Philadelphia and New York. It was through his prodding that the preachers began to spread out to other places in the colonies. Pilmore made a lengthy and important journey for Methodism through Pennsylvania, Maryland, Virginia, North and South Carolina, and Georgia. His southern journey began May 26, 1772, and continued until his return to St. George's Meeting House in June 1773.

Pilmore's Southern Journey and Its Importance

The importance of Pilmore's travels cannot be overestimated. First and most important, he gave the Methodist people in America a sense of oneness with all Methodists everywhere. Having been sent to America by John Wesley, he tied the Methodist societies to Wesley's leadership. Second, by his brotherly manner and able preaching, he made many friends for the Methodist movement. In addition, he organized a number of new societies including one in Baltimore and another in Norfolk. He preached not only in churches but also in a playhouse, under a tree, in a courthouse, and in a tavern—wherever he could secure a hearing. By his evangelical fervor, he proved the importance and power of Methodism's message.

II. Events Leading to a New Church—1773 to 1784

When Pilmore returned to Philadelphia in 1773, he discovered that Wesley had sent two more missionaries to America—Thomas Rankin and George Shadford. Originally, as we have seen, Wesley appointed Boardman leader of the American work; then he replaced Boardman by Asbury; now he replaced Asbury by Rankin, appointing him his general assistant.

First Conference of American Methodist Preachers

One of Rankin's first official acts in 1773 was to call a conference at St. George's, Philadelphia, of all the Methodist preachers in America. Ten preachers attended. The business centered in four important decisions. The *first* action united all Methodists in America under the spiritual leadership of John Wesley. The *second* action forbade the preachers to administer the sacraments because they were unordained. This was directed specifically at Strawbridge who was administering the sacraments and who continued, in spite of this ruling, to administer them until his death in 1781. The *third* action stated, "None of the preachers in America to reprint any of Mr. Wesley's books without his authority (when it can be gotten) and the consent of the brethren"—a prohibition made necessary by the activities of Robert Williams, a Methodist preacher who had come to America on his own initiative and who had been reprinting some of Wesley's hymns and books. The action was important because it brought the publishing business under the authority of the conference and was the first step toward establishing the control of the conference over all the future agencies of the church. The *fourth* action served to tighten the discipline of Methodism. Only society members were permitted to attend society meetings and love feast services, although visitors were permitted from time to time. Everyone, of course, was invited to attend the general preaching services. In addition, it was agreed that each pastor was to give an account of his work every six months. In time, this became the statistical report which is part of every annual conference of Methodism.

In 1773 membership statistics were as follows: New York 180, Philadelphia 180, New Jersey 200, Maryland 500, and Virginia 100; total 1,160. These members were serious-minded persons—ones who desired to be a "peculiar people." To that end the Methodist men usually wore shad-breasted coats and low-crowned hats; the women wore plain black bonnets—no white dresses, no jewelry, no rings. The men did not powder or tie back their hair, but arranged it in long locks combed straight down. The women had neither curls, side locks nor lace. The preachers usually wore parson-gray suits much like the Quakers; but, wishing to be distinguished from them, they wore collars on their coats and used a variety of drab colors, avoiding only the brighter materials. The dress of the United Brethren was as plain as that of the Methodists.

Wesley continued to appoint preachers to America until 1775, when the strained relations between the colonists and the mother country made this impractical. Eight preachers in all were officially sent by Wesley in addition to those who came on their own initiative. For the most part, their work was exceedingly effective. In the ensuing years, however, a series of crises threatened the entire Methodist movement.

Political Crisis—The Revolutionary War

One of the crises which threatened American Methodism was the Revolutionary War. It was commonly known that American Methodism looked for its leadership to John Wesley, who supported the right of Parliament to tax the colonies. This in itself caused the movement to be suspect by the rebellious colonists. Wesley, who advised his preachers in America to follow a neutral course, did not follow his own advice. In 1775 he extracted the main arguments of Samuel Johnson's *Taxation No Tyranny* and issued them in a pamphlet entitled *A Calm Address to Our American Colonies.* Unfortunately, to tell the Americans that they had "ceded to the King and Parliament, the power of disposing, without their consent, of both their lives, liberties and properties," was the surest way of alienating their allegiance and respect. As a result, the Methodists in America became the objects of suspicion, and the lives of some of the preachers and laity were seriously endangered.

Second, although some Methodists actively supported the revolutionary cause, a number of Methodist preachers refused for conscientious reasons to bear arms. In addition, all the preachers Wesley had sent to America returned home except two—Francis Asbury and James Dempster, who became a Presbyterian. Before leaving the country, moreover, some of the preachers spoke out strongly against the revolution.

Because a number of colonies demanded that their citizens take an oath of allegiance including the willingness to bear arms, Asbury took refuge for about two years at the home of Judge Thomas White near Dover, Delaware, where the oath of allegiance did not include this objectionable statement. Many Methodist preachers were persecuted simply because they were Methodists.

Eventually the opposition to Methodism died down. This may have been due partly to the patience and sincerity of the Methodists under persecution. It may also have been because of a letter written by Asbury to Rankin in 1777, which sometime later fell into the hands of American officers. In the letter Asbury stated that he believed the Americans would become a free and independent nation, and that he, himself, was knit in affection to too many of them to leave.

Persecution seldom destroys a religious movement. More often it causes it to grow. Although Methodism declined in some places, particularly New York, in most colonies it continued to grow. From 1776 to 1783 the membership of Methodism almost tripled to a total of 13,740.

In 1774 Otterbein became pastor of a German Reformed Church in Baltimore where he served for nearly forty years while continuing his work with Boehm. Since most of their work lay in the interior of Pennsylvania, Maryland, and Virginia the war had little effect on their ministries. However, informal annual conferences held by Otterbein and Boehm with their preachers were halted by the war.

Spiritual Crisis—The Sacramental Controversy

Another crisis faced Methodism during the years of the American Revolution. It was caused in part by the fact that, with the coming of the war, many Anglican priests returned to England or went to Canada. Since the Methodist preachers were unordained, this meant that baptism and communion could not be provided for large numbers of Methodists. Some of the people and preachers believed that if the preachers were good enough to preach they should be considered good enough to administer the sacraments. At one point, some of the stronger preachers in the southern colonies ordained one another; but Asbury and the northern preachers were opposed to this method of providing the sacraments and looked upon these preachers as having left Methodism.

*E*stimates vary of how many people in Britain's American colonies desired independence when the Declaration of Independence was signed, but scholars agree it was a minority. Hence, leaders of the rebellion had to win over doubting individuals and convince the colonies from New England to Georgia to hang together in the fight for independence. One of their pieces of propaganda was the "Join or Die" serpent.

The matter was finally settled in 1780. After conducting a confere nce in the north which supported his position, Asbury made his way to Manakintown, Virginia, where the dissidents were meeting. They were led by powerful men including James O'Kelly, later the leader of a schism. For some time the meeting was deadlocked, and then quite unexpectedly the preachers agreed on a compromise. The conference decided to resume for one year the former practice of not administering the sacraments on condition that Asbury would write to Wesley for guidance. It was not until four years later, however, that Wesley arrived at a solution to the problem.

Wesley's Plan for American Methodism

Through his reading of Lord Peter King's account of the early Christian church, Wesley had come to the conclusion that both bishops and ministers have the right to ordain. Although still believing that Methodists should never leave the Church of England, he realized that the situation in America was different from that at home. America had won political independence. The Anglican Church, furthermore, had no bishops in America, and many of its parishes were without priests. Thus in America, the church to which the Methodists might cling was rapidly declining. In addition, Wesley had sought without success to have one person ordained for America by an Anglican bishop. In Wesley's eyes, therefore, the situation in America was an emergency that called for radical measures.

Wesley discussed the matter with numerous persons, including Thomas Coke, a keen-minded priest in the Church of England. In the end, Wesley himself made the decision. At about four o'clock in the morning of September 1, 1784, Wesley, assisted by Thomas Creighton, an Anglican priest, ordained Richard Whatcoat and Thomas Vasey as deacons; the next morning, he and Creighton ordained Whatcoat and Vasey as elders and Thomas Coke as superintendent for the work in America.

On September 18, 1784, the three ordained men set sail for America, armed with documents and a carton of unbound hymn books and prayer books. The documents included Wesley's certificate of ordination setting apart Thomas Coke as superintendent. It is considered the basic document on which Methodist ordination rests. A second document was a letter from Wesley addressed to "Dr. Coke, Mr. Asbury and our Brethren in America." The letter outlines the "uncommon train of providence" that led Wesley to act. It tells how Wesley came to the conclusion that bishops and ministers are of the same order with the same right to ordain. Pointing to the emergency situation in America, Wesley writes, "I have accordingly appointed Dr. Coke and Mr. Francis Asbury to be joint superintendents over our brethren in North America . . . and I have prepared a liturgy little differing from that of the Church of England . . . I also advise the elders to administer the Supper of the Lord on every Lord's Day." Included with the prayer book, called *The Sunday Service of the Methodists in North America*, was Wesley's reduction of the Thirty-Nine Articles of Religion of the Anglican Church to twenty-four. He closes by challenging anyone to "point out a more rational and scriptural way of feeding and guiding these poor sheep in the wilderness . . ."

Coke, Whatcoat, and Vasey arrived in New York and then proceeded to Philadelphia where they publicly revealed Wesley's plan for the American Methodist churches. From Philadelphia they went to Barratt's Chapel in Delaware where they met Francis Asbury. It was agreed that a meeting of the preachers should be called, and Freeborn Garrettson was commissioned to notify all the preachers to attend a conference during the Christmas season at Lovely Lane Chapel in Baltimore. A large percentage of the preachers were present.

The Christmas Conference—1784

The conference took a series of important actions. First, the Methodist movement was organized into a church named the Methodist Episcopal Church in America. Second, Asbury, who refused to accept Wesley's appointment as a superintendent unless elected by the preachers, was unanimously voted into the office of superintendent. Later, the term "bishop" came to be used, a fact that displeased Wesley greatly. It is significant that when Asbury was to be ordained he requested that his friend William Otterbein assist in the ordination. Otterbein would later become co-founder of the Church of the United Brethren in Christ.

Third, a form of discipline was adopted, along with Wesley's abridgment of the thirty-nine Anglican articles of religion to twenty-four. The conference added a twenty-fifth article relating to "Rulers of the United States of America." The preachers had always accepted Wesley's *Sermons* and his *Notes upon the New Testament* as their doctrinal standards; now they added the articles of religion. *The Sunday Service,* Wesley's prayer book, was never extensively used. Most of the preachers believed "that they could pray better, and with more devotion while their eyes were shut, than they could with their eyes open."

The new church followed its own more informal liturgy for communion. Its occasional services included the Watchnight Service, the Covenant Service, and the Love Feast. The Watchnight Service, with its strong emphasis on singing, prayer, testimony, and rededication, came to be used on New Year's Eve. The Love Feast centered in the breaking

*T*he organizing conference of the Methodist Episcopal
Church in America was held at Lovely Lane Chapel in
Baltimore during the Christmas season of 1784. A number of
deacons and elders were ordained, and Francis Asbury was
elected to supervise the circuit-riding preachers. Philip William
Otterbein, co-founder of the Church of the United Brethren in
Christ, assisted in the act of setting Asbury apart for his work
as superintendent.

and distribution of bread and the passing of two-handled mugs of water from which all drank. Singing, testimony, and preaching also characterized this service. The new church preferred fervent preaching and lusty singing to a formal liturgy.

Fourth, the Christmas Conference passed a rule forbidding the preachers to use intoxicating liquors except for medicinal purposes.

Fifth, a rule was passed to stamp out the abomination of slavery. Wesley planted opposition to slavery deep within Methodism. He had been an effective voice against it in England when in 1774 he published his powerful pamphlet *Thoughts Upon Slavery*. Thomas Coke on several occasions endangered his life in America by his forthright preaching against slavery. However, the rule was short-lived, being offensive to most of the southern Methodists. It is difficult to imagine what would have happened had the church continued its strong stand against slavery. At any rate, the church turned a corner when it eventually allowed individual conferences to decide the issue.

The Christmas Conference adopted a form of church government that gave bishops a place of central importance. In a resolution it stated that the church's purpose was "to reform the continent and to spread scriptural holiness through these lands." It agreed on an action, later ignored, to obey the commands of Wesley during his lifetime. Approval was given to establish a college, named Cokesbury after the two bishops. Probably thirteen persons were ordained as elders and fourteen as deacons. For the first time in its history, American Methodism had its own ordained clergy. In addition, at the earnest request of William Black, a Wesleyan preacher from Nova Scotia, Freeborn Garrettson and James Cromwell were sent as missionaries to eastern Canada. In 1800 the work was taken over by the Wesleyan

Methodists of England. Jeremiah Lambert and John Baxter were assigned to Antigua in the Caribbean.

At least one, and possibly two, blacks attended the conference—Harry Hosier and Richard Allen. They were symbolic of the work that Methodism had been doing among the blacks. A black girl was a member of the class formed in 1766 by Philip Embury in New York. Pilmore writes of a Love Feast where blacks and whites met together, testified, and broke bread together. Francis Asbury was particularly sensitive to the needs of the blacks and made every effort to bring them the gospel.

Hosier, often called "Black Harry," was probably the most gifted early black preacher produced by Methodism. He served occasionally as a traveling companion to both Thomas Coke and Francis Asbury. Coke spoke of him as one of the best preachers in the world, high praise from a person of Coke's attainments and judgment.

Richard Allen received his license to preach from Old St. George's in Philadelphia in 1784. He was ordained a deacon by Asbury in 1799. Allen was never ordained an elder in the Methodist Episcopal Church.

III. The Churches of United Methodism and Their Early Progress—1784 to 1816

The Evangelical Association

Jacob Albright

An exceedingly important phase of the history of The United Methodist Church began in 1796 with the preaching of Jacob Albright among the Germans of Pennsylvania. The Albright family had emigrated from Germany in 1732 and settled in a farming district of eastern Pennsylvania. Jacob was born May 1, 1759, and received the bare rudiments of an education, learning to read and write both in German and English. He was active in the Pennsylvania Militia during the Revolutionary War, and in 1785, after his marriage to Catherine Cope, a member of the Reformed Church, he settled on a farm in Pennsylvania's Lancaster County and united with a Lutheran church. His farm contained valuable clay and limestone deposits, and Albright founded a tile factory. Because of the integrity of his work and his business ethics, he became known as "the Honest Tilemaker."

When several of Albright's children died in 1790, he was led to serious thoughts about his religious life through the preaching of Anthony Houtz, a Reformed pastor who conducted the funeral services for the children. In 1791, Adam Riegel, a member of the United Brethren in Christ, aided Albright in his search for an evangelical religious experience.

Having found peace with God, Albright began preaching among the Pennsylvania Germans in 1796. He first traveled in southeastern Pennsylvania, then north and west, and still later into Maryland and Virginia. His evangelical preaching, with its emphasis on the need for a change of heart rather than on greater participation in the forms and ceremonies of the church, stirred up opposition among the Reformed and Lutheran people. On several occasions his life was endangered, and he was severely beaten. Nevertheless, by 1800 he had formed three societies in southeastern Pennsylvania, each with a membership of about twenty.

Growth and Development

In 1803 Albright gathered his followers together for a two-day meeting at the home of Samuel Liesser in Berks County, Pennsylvania. "Albright's People," as some termed them, declared themselves an ecclesiastical organization, stated that the Scriptures were to be their rule and guide in faith and practice, and ordained Albright as their pastor, an ordination possibly by resolution rather than by the laying on of hands.

The first annual conference of Albright's People was held in mid-November 1807 at the home of Samuel Becker with twenty-eight persons in attendance, including five itinerant and three local preachers. The membership numbered well over two hundred. The conference decided to prepare a Discipline based upon the *Discipline of the Methodist Episcopal Church,* and it adopted the name, The Newly-Formed Methodist Connection. One of the most important actions of the conference was the election of Jacob Albright as bishop of the new denomination, a title bestowed by vote. Some months later, May 18, 1808, Albright died.

After Albright's death the work was ably led by George

Miller, who edited the first Discipline of the denomination, adopted in 1809. It was based largely on a German translation of the *Discipline of the Methodist Episcopal Church*. Miller died of a heart attack in 1816.

Another leader, John Dreisbach, received his license to preach when he was seventeen years old. Largely self-educated, he was bilingual, speaking both English and German fluently, and he had a proficient knowledge of the sermons of John Wesley. He was also a gifted writer, administrator, and preacher. Francis Asbury coveted him for the Methodist Episcopal Church, and in 1810 strove earnestly to persuade Dreisbach to leave the Evangelicals for the Methodists but was unsuccessful.

Dreisbach was secretary of the annual conference from 1809 to 1812. His brethren recognized his unusual gifts for leadership and, after serving as presiding officer at two annual conferences, he was elected presiding elder in 1814. In this capacity he presided at the first General Conference in 1816.

At this conference the group took the name, the Evangelical Association. In two other important actions the General Conference chose Solomon Miller as superintendent of the printing facilities that had been established at New Berlin, Pennsylvania, and considered a proposal to unite the Evangelical Association and the Church of the United Brethren in Christ, but nothing came of the move for union at that time.

It is a matter for speculation why neither the Evangelical leaders not their followers were willing to call their new denomination a church. This reluctance may be attributed to Albright's emphasis on the need for a change of heart rather than a reliance on church forms and ceremonies for an assurance of salvation.

The Church of the United Brethren in Christ

Organization
The Church of the United Brethren in Christ met for organization on September 25, 1800, when a group of thirteen or fourteen preachers and other followers of Otterbein and Boehm gathered at the home of Frederick Kemp, about a mile west of Frederick, Maryland. Otterbein and Boehm were elected bishops; the name of the denomination was chosen, the Church of the United Brethren in Christ, and it was agreed to make a German translation of the *Discipline of the Methodist Episcopal Church*. The full name of the denomination was not widely used at first and did not become the legal title of the church until 1890. The Methodist Episcopal Discipline was translated into German, but it was never officially adopted and the church made little use of it.

Expansion
New leadership began to appear in persons like George Adam Geeting, Christopher Grosh, and Christian Newcomer; and the work began to spread westward into Ohio, Kentucky, and Indiana, leading to the formation of a western conference. When preachers in the west grew weary of being ignored by sister denominations because they lacked ordination, Otterbein decided to act. He ordained Christian Newcomer, Joseph Hoffman, and Frederick Shaffer on October 2, 1813, assisted by William Ryland, an elder in the Methodist Episcopal Church.

The first General Conference of the new denomination was held in June 1815. By this time both Otterbein and Boehm were dead—Boehm having died in 1812, Otterbein in 1813. Otterbein never resigned from the German Reformed Church, just as Wesley never left the Anglican Church. Newcomer, who had been elected a bishop in 1813 and again in 1814, presided over the conference. A brief Confession of Faith was adopted. It has seven paragraphs, four based upon the Apostles' Creed and the remainder on the Bible. The Discipline was somewhat enlarged, and a denominational hymnal was approved. The eastern and western conferences were formally recognized, and it was agreed that the General Conference should meet every four years, at which time bishops were to be elected.

Some Characteristics of the Churches

Doctrines and Practices

It is significant that Methodists, United Brethren, and Evangelicals all emphasized the doctrine of justification by faith alone and Christian perfection. The main task of the circuit rider was the saving of souls. Not much emphasis was placed upon social concerns or politics. This is strange since John Wesley believed that every saved person should be a useful member of society, which meant becoming involved in social action and having a grasp on the political events of the day. In America, Asbury stayed clear of politics and the social order. One can read his journal and letters and find almost no reference to the Revolutionary War or the War of 1812, or to other political and social events of his era.

Methodist circuit riders, however, did proclaim the rules for a Methodist as set down by John Wesley, and to some degree these touched upon social problems—smuggling, gambling, drinking, slave-holding, and other practices. The only thing done on anything like a national level in the political field was when the Methodist Episcopal conference directed Asbury and Coke in 1789 to extend the congratulations of the church to George Washington, the newly elected President of the United States, and to assure him of its loyalty to the Constitution.

None of the denominations had an educated ministry. It is true that during these early years each denomination sought gradually to lift the general standards of education among its preachers, and it is also true that the organizing conference of the Methodist Episcopal Church in 1784 voted to erect a college—Cokesbury; but when it burned down Asbury seemed more relieved than distressed. In 1796 it was relocated in Baltimore where, in the same year, it again burned. Asbury supported the organization of academies in some states, but it was left to a later leadership to create an educated ministry.

On the other hand, from their beginnings in America, Methodists published the religious tracts of John Wesley and other religious material. John Dickins was appointed first Book Editor of the Methodist Episcopal Church in 1789, and he founded the Book Concern at St. George's in Philadelphia. Early in their history also, United Brethren and Evangelicals became interested in publishing.

The three denominations did not trust the laity sufficiently to allot them a role in ruling the churches. No lay person was a voting member of either the general or annual conferences. No women were ordained during this period, although Joseph Pilmore appointed Mary Thorne as the first female class leader in American Methodism; later she returned to England and was forgotten. Asbury looked upon women with suspicion. He preferred a celibate ministry, and, although he could not prevent his ministers from marrying, he once made a sarcastic comment about those men who had to run home every night to their "dears." Dreisbach, by contrast, was twice married and often spoke of how his wives helped him in his ministry. He had eleven children by his two wives and enjoyed a happy home life.

The men and women of the three churches dressed very simply, and their meetinghouses continued to be plain, unadorned structures. For many years organs as well as steeples for the churches were taboo.

Splits and Schisms

There was a lack of democracy particularly in the Methodist Episcopal Church, where it was more pronounced than in the Evangelical and United Brethren churches. As a result, several splits occurred in the last decade of the eighteenth century and the first third of the nineteenth that weakened the Methodists.

The first serious split occurred when Asbury refused to appoint William Hammett, a British pioneer of West Indian Methodism, to the Methodist church in Charleston, South Carolina, the members of which were clamoring for his appointment. Asbury insisted on the right of the bishop to fix the appointments and strongly opposed Hammett's desire to remain at one church for a prolonged period. Hammett left the church in 1791 and erected Trinity Church in Charleston, taking a large number of Methodists with him. He called the new denomination the Primitive Methodist Church, but when he died in 1803 the denomination died with him.

The O'Kelly schism in 1792 followed a similar pattern. James O'Kelly led a faction that insisted every preacher should have the right of appeal to the conference if he were dissatisfied with his appointment. This demand is evidence of a deep-rooted dissatisfaction with the growing power of the episcopacy, and particularly the authority of Francis Asbury. However, the O'Kelly dissidents were unable to carry their point, so they left the Methodist Episcopal Church and formed the Republican Methodist Church. Its greatest strength lay in the border counties of North Carolina and Virginia. Although O'Kelly drew between 15 and 20 percent of its members away from the Methodist Episcopal Church, his movement had lost its momentum by 1801, and he changed the name of the denomination to the Christian Church. Through divisions and subdivisions, it gradually dwindled away.

Methodist work among the blacks, though generally successful, was also marred by schism. Richard Allen of Philadelphia and Daniel Coker of Baltimore both experienced discrimination against blacks in the Methodist Episcopal Church. Allen, writing about the incident when he was an old man, indicates that in 1787 an attempt was made during a morning service forcibly to move him and several of his friends to a segregated part of St. George's Church. After prayer they left the church, although Allen maintained a nominal connection with the Methodist Episcopal Church until 1816. When he built the forerunner of what is now Mother Bethel Church in Philadelphia, he called upon Francis Asbury and John Dickins, then pastor of Old St. George's, to assist with the dedication. In 1816, when Allen issued an invitation to other African churches in the country to form an ecclesiastical pact, representatives came from Baltimore, Maryland; Wilmington, Delaware; Attleborough, Pennsylvania; Salem, New Jersey; and, of course, Philadelphia. Out of their meeting came the African Methodist Episcopal Church with Allen as its first bishop. The first Discipline of the church was largely patterned after the *Discipline of the Methodist Episcopal Church* and was published in 1817.

Many blacks remained faithful to the Methodist Episcopal Church. Some formed separate societies; the oldest of these is Zoar United Methodist Church founded in Philadelphia in 1794.

During this period two other black denominations were organized—the African Methodist Episcopal Zion Church and the Union Church of Africans. The Zion group came

*J*ohn Wesley planted opposition to slavery deep in Methodism. Writing just days before he died to William Wilberforce, British anti-slave-trade advocate, Wesley said, "Go on, in the name of God, and in the power of his might, till even American slavery, the vilest that ever saw the sun, shall vanish before it." The 1784 Discipline of the Methodist Episcopal Church, following Wesley's lead, gave Methodists two choices: free their slaves or leave the church.

Question 42
What methods can we take to extirpate slavery?

Answer:
1. Every member of our society who has slaves in his possession, shall, within twelve months after notice given to him, legally execute and record an instrument, whereby he emancipates and sets free every slave in his possession

from churches in New Haven, Philadelphia, Long Island, and New York and was organized in 1821.

The Union Church of Africans began in Wilmington, Delaware, the result of a split from the Methodist Episcopal Church led by Peter Spencer. In 1813 he organized his followers and other groups into the African Union Church. His was the first separate black denomination in America. He could not be persuaded by Richard Allen to merge with the African Methodist Episcopal Church in 1816.

The Churches Take Shape

By the beginning of the nineteenth century the Methodists, the Evangelicals, and the United Brethren had all changed from religious movements into full-blown churches with an ordained clergy, a Confession of Faith, a Discipline, and an organization. When the Methodist Episcopal Church was organized in 1784, it was composed of local societies or individual churches, which in turn were divided into classes or small groups for spiritual growth. Churches were governed by quarterly conferences over which a presiding elder or district superintendent presided. The churches, through their pastors, were also a part of a larger body termed an annual conference. A bishop presided at the annual conference and ended the sessions by fixing the pastoral appointments. When the United Brethren and the Evangelicals organized, they followed the basic pattern of the Methodists, although each church had distinctive ways of handling bishops, district superintendents, and ordained ministers.

Every four years, from 1792, the preachers in the Methodist Episcopal Church gathered for a General Conference, the highest legislative body of the church. The first General Conference of the United Brethren was held in 1815, and the first in the Evangelical Association in 1816. In 1808 the

Methodist Episcopal Church decided that the General Conference should be a delegated body with representatives from each annual conference. In the Church of the United Brethren this was done at the first General Conference in 1815, but it was not a practice in the Evangelical Association until 1839.

The 1808 General Conference of the Methodists adopted a constitution for the church that included six restrictive rules. The most important of these made it impossible for the General Conference to alter the doctrines of the church, to do away with the episcopacy, or to appropriate the proceeds of the Book Concern for any purpose other than that of providing benefits for retired preachers and their families.

In 1815 the General Conference of the United Brethren Church provided for the election of bishops with a term of four years, but with the opportunity for re-election; provided for one ordination, that of elder; and expressly forbade the General Conference from taking any action "which shall abolish or do away with the itinerant plan." In many ways, however, the three churches were showing remarkable similarity as they took shape.

Unfortunately, none of the churches did much work among the Indians. In 1789 only three Indians are recorded as members of the Methodist Episcopal Church. In that year Thomas Coke resolved to carry on a mission to the Indians but never successfully pursued his goal. Methodists did not begin work among the Indians until 1815 or 1816, when John Stewart, a mulatto, began his work among the Wyandot Indians in Ohio.

During these years an attempt was also made at union between the Methodist Episcopal and the United Brethren churches and between the Evangelicals and the United Brethren but nothing came of these efforts at that time.

Camp Meetings and Revivalism

At the turn of the century camp meetings emerged, the first recorded one being held during July 1800 in Kentucky. The moving spirits were two brothers—John and William McGee—the former a Methodist local preacher, the latter a Presbyterian clergyman. Spreading rapidly the movement was quickly systematized into orderly gatherings, with persons living in tents and wagons and with supervisors always at hand to ensure the safety of the congregation from intruders and to maintain a high level of morality among the participants. The meetings sometimes lasted for several weeks and provided fellowship and religious teaching for vast numbers of people. They were often highly emotional gatherings; sometimes people fainted, experienced the shakes, and some got converted.

Last Days of Otterbein, Boehm, and Asbury

Martin Boehm died on March 23, 1812, after a six-day illness. Francis Asbury, in response to a strong inner prompting, had been on his way to visit Boehm when he received word of his death.

Otterbein died peacefully at Baltimore November 17, 1813. When he heard of Otterbein's passing, Asbury said, "Great and good man of God! An honor to his church and country. One of the greatest scholars and divines that ever came to America, or born in it."

Francis Asbury attended his last conference in October 1815. By this time Richard Whatcoat had been elected a bishop in 1800 and had died in 1806. William McKendree, the first native American bishop, had been elected in 1808. Asbury died on Sunday afternoon, March 31, 1816, while trying in a delirium to receive a missionary offering.

Jacob Albright, as we have noted, had died May 18,

1808. The four great leaders of these early churches died within a decade.

The first epoch in the history of the Methodist Episcopal Church, the Church of the United Brethren in Christ, and the Evangelical Association had come to a close. The growth, expansion, and gains of the churches had been remarkable. Evangelistic fervor was at a great height, and in 1814, with the closing of the War of 1812 and the opening of the west, a new era was beginning for the churches. The future held hope and challenge. The churches were on the march.

Part Two

The Nineteenth Century

by Charles Yrigoyen, Jr.

*W*orship in Evangelical, United Brethren, and Methodist churches during the nineteenth century owed much to camp meetings. It was informal and spirited, often highly emotional, with emphasis placed on fiery preaching, extemporaneous praying, joyful singing, and passionate testifying. People responded to such services by rolling, twitching, fainting, and making commitments to Christ that issued in transformed living.

I. Growth and Development— 1816 to 1843

The first half of the nineteenth century provided the opportunity for the American people to acquire an appreciation for the potential of their land, its resources and the talents of its populace. When Francis Asbury died in 1816, the young nation was just beginning to realize its promise. It was entering a period of territorial expansion, agricultural and industrial development, and population growth.

The land was suitable for successful farming and abundant with raw materials for manufacturing. Inventions and improvements in existing machinery and tools resulted in larger productivity on farms and in factories. The invention of the steel plow, the reaper, and the thresher represented major advances in agricultural technology. The creation of the telegraph and the harnessing of water and steam power also proved significant for the nation's life. Canals, turnpikes, railroads, and steamboats opened routes for settlers, travelers, and goods. Despite the financial panics of 1819 and 1837 the nation was progressing. Its people were optimistic. It was the age of the Monroe Doctrine and Jacksonian Democracy. Immigration from England and Europe rose dramatically. The population grew from 9 million in 1815 to over 23 million in 1850. For the adventuresome there was a seemingly limitless frontier to explore and settle. The American people were developing a very positive attitude about themselves, their role as a national power and their future.

The Second Great Awakening and Social Reform

The most prominent religious development in early nineteenth-century America was the Second Great Awakening. This movement of religious fervor spread across the nation, reaching the midpoint of its life about the time of Asbury's death. While its intensity and accompanying phenomena varied in different sections of the nation, its major thrust was to convert sinners. In revivals and camp meetings throughout the country, there was an unprecedented effort to bring the wayward to an experience of salvation.

Thousands of people under the direction of preachers and lay leaders experienced conversion. This transformation usually consisted of four stages. First, the prospect became convinced of his or her guilt as a sinner. Second, there was a feeling of despair. The sinner deserved God's wrathful punishment. Third, there was hope. God was gracious. He was always ready to forgive the penitent sinner and to restore the sinner to a proper relationship with him through faith in Christ. Finally, there was an experience of assurance. Guilt, despair, and hope gave way to the joy of salvation experienced in the sinner's life. This type of conversion was the goal of the revival and the camp meeting.

There were several important consequences of the Second Awakening. It stirred theological disagreement. Some vehemently criticized it as superficial, individualistic, and emotionally excessive. Some critics preferred a more reasoned religion; others disliked the new revivalistic techniques associated with it. They desired more traditional and formal religious expressions. The Awakening led to prorevivalist and antirevivalist parties in some of the denominations. Churches, however, which had historically been sympathetic to an experiential approach to Christianity, such as the Methodists, the Evangelical Association, and the United Brethren in Christ, witnessed remarkable growth in conversions, membership, and new congregations. Other American Protestant bodies, notably the Presbyterians and Baptists, also grew rapidly during the high tide of the movement. The Awakening envisioned more than converted individuals; it looked forward to a reformed society as well. Hoping to Christianize every aspect of American life, thousands of evangelical Protestants organized voluntary societies to attack the social evils of the young nation. These societies sprang up wherever interest in their cause could be created. Their memberships were constituted without regard for an individual's denominational affiliation. They were often effectively organized into local, state, and national structures. In conventions and rallies and through the publication and distribution of literature, they attempted to mold public opinion and governmental policy in accordance with their reforms. Temperance groups, Bible and tract societies, benevolent associations to aid the poor, women's rights organizations, and abolitionist societies were but a few of the components of this "moral militia." Many Protestants believed that the dream of the Puritan forefathers of a Christian America was soon to be realized. Revivalism and social reform were the means by which it would be attained. The spiritual kin of the Wesleys, Albright, and Otterbein were prepared to participate.

Keys to Continued Growth

The years 1816 through 1843 were marked by significant growth in each of the churches that presently compose United Methodism. The Methodists numbered about one million by 1843. The Evangelical Association reported more than a 500 percent increase in members. The United Brethren likewise witnessed a large rise in membership. The churches could also boast about the establishment of new congregations and swelling ministerial ranks. How can we account for this extraordinary growth? Several factors may explain it. Among the most important are: one, the unusual dedication of the preachers and laity; two, a form of organization suited to the conditions of the time; and three, the extension of the ministries of the Evangelical Association and the United Brethren Church to English-speaking people.

Dedication

Virtually all the preachers in these churches were convinced that they were called of God to preach. This call came to them in a variety of ways, and it was the principal motivation for their ministry in settled communities or sparsely settled frontier areas. Those who answered the call were soon aware that theirs was a demanding and disciplined vocation. They were expected to preach, organize classes, visit the sick, stir up the weak in faith, encourage and support the faithful, read and study the Scriptures and other edifying literature, and set an example for the laity. Many preachers, particularly on the frontier, were often required to function in severely adverse geographical and weather conditions. Furthermore, many of them encountered hostility from those belonging to other churches who resented their presence as well as from unbelievers who were equally antagonistic. The work was demanding! The wages were modest. In 1816 the preachers of the Evangelical Association were paid $60 per year plus travel expenses. As late as 1843 their annual wage was $100 if single, $200 if married, and an additional $25 for each child under 14 years of age. Salaries among the Methodists and United Brethren were comparable. Many of the clergy supplemented their income by acting as agents for the sale of books and literature from their publishing houses. Even this, however, resulted in very little additional revenue. Among the earlier preachers, marriage was discouraged because of the low wages and the extended absences caused by riding a circuit of preaching places.

Rigid standards of conduct for the laity were enforced in the churches. Methodism had formulated rigorous principles for clergy and laity in the General Rules adopted at the Christmas Conference in 1784. Methodists were urged to do no harm and to avoid evil of every kind. Included in this prohibition were profaning the sabbath, drunkenness, wearing gold and costly apparel, fighting and quarreling, singing songs and reading books that did not lead to the knowledge and love of God, and "laying up treasures upon earth." They were also expected to do good. Feeding the hungry, clothing the naked, visiting the sick and imprisoned, "denying themselves, and taking up their cross daily" were among the positive disciplines Methodists were to practice. They were also required to observe "all the ordinances of God," such as attendance at public worship and the Lord's Supper, private prayer, fasting, and Bible study. Similar standards probably kept membership lower than it might have been otherwise among the Evangelicals and the United Brethren. The laity, as much as the clergy, were expected to be converted, committed, and disciplined participants in the churches to which they belonged. Together they rejoiced in a fellowship that was mutually beneficial.

Organization

A second important factor in the expansion of the churches was the manner in which they were organized. The Wesleyan model of small groups called classes was especially useful in rural and frontier regions. Classes ranged in membership from three or four persons up to fifty or more. Each class was visited as regularly as possible by a circuit preacher. He appointed a class leader, a lay person, who presided over a weekly meeting of the membership. Prayer, study, admonition, and mutual encouragement forged a bond which, between the preacher's sometimes infrequent visits, kept the faithful together and growing. The class meeting system was extensively and effectively employed in the Evangelical Association and the United Brethren Church as well as in Methodism.

Each of the churches also had developed a structure with established patterns of authority and responsibility, thus making it possible to monitor progress, marshal resources, and map strategy. For example, general and annual conferences had been created to legislate policy, and bishops were elected to implement the legislation.

Language Restrictions

A third growth factor was expansion into work among English-speaking people by the Evangelicals and the United Brethren. The ministry of each of these churches before 1816 was confined almost exclusively to the German-speaking population. Then it became evident to many of their leaders that they could effectively enlarge their ministry by reaching out to those who spoke English. Furthermore, many suspected that the use of the German language might decline as the generations passed. After considerable debate and deliberation, work among the English-speaking began. John McNamar, licensed in 1813, was the first English-language preacher among the United Brethren. Others were licensed shortly thereafter.

Between 1820 and 1850 there was much agitation within the Evangelical Association to expand its ministry to the English-speaking. By 1830 there were several English-language preachers in the church. Fearful that the German-language base of the church would be eroded, however, the General Conference of 1830 held that only preachers with some knowledge of German were acceptable for licensing. This restriction may have hampered the general growth of the

Evangelical Association until 1843 when the General Conference decided to give more attention to work among English-speaking people. Ironically, Methodism, whose ministry was almost solely to the English-speaking, began work among the German-speaking in the 1830s.

Worship, Education, Missions, and Publication

Many of the most important developments in the churches during the 1816–1843 period involved four areas: worship, education and the Sunday school, missions, and publication. Each of these deserves some attention.

Worship

Worship was of central importance. Scripture reading, preaching, exhorting, praying, and singing were prominent when the people gathered in homes, church buildings, and camp meetings. Hymn singing was very popular. Hymns were often taught by the preacher or song leader who "lined" them for the congregation. The leader spoke or sang a line that was then sung by the assembly until a hymn became familiar. Hymn books were also available. The focal point of worship was the sermon. It was based upon a passage of scripture and was usually preached with verve and conviction. It was commonplace for the sermon or service to end with a call for repentance, acceptance of Christ, and an invitation to join the church.

Adult and infant baptism were practiced in all three churches, and suitable baptismal rituals were provided in their Disciplines. The mode of baptism varied widely; immersion, pouring, and sprinkling were employed. The Lord's Supper was highly esteemed, though it was usually celebrated infrequently. Methodists, for example, generally held quarterly observances of the Lord's Supper, perhaps because of the scarcity of clergy to administer it. Each church prescribed a ritual by which it was to be celebrated, but some ministers preferred to follow their own forms. Among Methodists the use of wine was common, although some dissent about this was beginning to appear due to the influence of the temperance movement. Other worship practices among the Methodists included love feasts, prayer meetings, watch nights, and congregational fasts. The United Brethren occasionally held footwashing services.

The churches became more active in the construction of meeting places, although classes continued to meet in private homes, and camp meeting grounds provided an earthy setting for revivals. The earliest meetinghouses were simple structures. Some were nothing more than large log cabins or frame buildings, especially on the frontier. In the more settled regions buildings were often erected following the Federal style of architecture. The dress of the clergy was usually plain and simple, but some Methodist preachers preferred to wear gowns.

Education

Education was another area of the churches' interest. All three churches promoted Sunday schools. The preachers of the Methodist Episcopal Church were ordered "to encourage the establishment and progress of Sunday schools" by the General Conference of 1824. Three years later the Methodist Sunday School Union was founded to promote the expansion of Sunday schools and to consolidate their strength as an integral part of the Methodist Episcopal Church. Its publishing house was directed to supply acceptable literature for the Sunday schools. It is believed that the first Sunday school of the Evangelical Association was organized in Lebanon, Pennsylvania, in 1832. The General Conference of 1835 resolved that "German Sabbath Schools" were to be established wherever possible. Gradually, the Sunday school

*B*y the third and fourth decades of the nineteenth century, the churches that now compose The United Methodist Church were sufficiently confident of their human talents and material resources to begin developing colleges, orphanages, mission boards, publishing houses, and agencies of moral reform in response to their understanding of Jesus' teachings.

movement grew in the Evangelical Association. It is more difficult to determine when the United Brethren began their Sunday school work. It may have been as early as 1820. The church encouraged the expansion of Sunday schools and provided materials for them through its publishing house. Secondary schools and colleges were also on this era's agenda. The Methodists instituted secondary schools such as Wesleyan Academy in Wilbraham, Massachusetts (1815), and a number of colleges. Among the latter were Randolph-Macon College in Virginia (1830), Wesleyan University in Connecticut (1831), and McKendree College in Illinois (1835). The United Brethren and the Evangelical Association discussed the matter of educational institutions. The United Brethren opened the first of several colleges, Otterbein University in Westerville, Ohio, in 1847. The Evangelical Association delayed the launching of a school until 1852 when it started Albright Seminary in New Berlin, Pennsylvania.

There was ample disagreement in the churches concerning the education of their ministers. Numerous reasons were offered in opposition to any formal theological education for "junior preachers." The call of God to the ministry was regarded as the only necessary preparation. Theological education would probably lessen the preacher's zeal for evangelism and personal piety. It might expose him to unorthodox views. It would cause divisiveness in the ministry between those who had been educated and those who had not. It took time from saving souls and threatened to create an intellectual gap between the clergy and laity. In spite of the opposition, however, there was some sentiment to institute an educational program that would ensure a more knowledgeable ministry. The 1816 General Conference of the Methodist Episcopal Church recommended that the annual conferences organize "a course of reading and study proper to be pursued by candidates for the ministry," but the proposal was not uniformly implemented. Some annual conferences developed effective study programs while others were lax. The 1843 General Conference of the Evangelical Association and the United Brethren General Conference of 1845 enacted legislation that established courses of study for their preachers. Theological seminaries were generally held in great disdain by all three churches, although a few voices advocated formal theological training. Some Methodists in New England, for example, succeeded in founding an institution for theological instruction. It opened in 1841 as the Newbury Biblical Institute in Newbury, Vermont.

Missions
Mission work represents the third principal activity of the period. The churches were interested in reaching the unconverted at home and abroad. Missionary societies were organized to develop strategies and provide funds for this work. In 1838 the German Evangelical Missionary Society of North America was begun under the sponsorship of the eastern conference of the Evangelical Association. Its purpose was "to make arrangements and provide means, to extend and promote the kingdom of God, by missionaries." One year later, believing that the whole church should participate in a formal mission program, the General Missionary Society of the Evangelical Association was formed. Women's auxiliaries of the General Society were organized in the same year. Mission work extended the ministry in the western as well as the eastern sections of the church. The Parent Missionary Society of the United Brethren in Christ was established by the 1841 General Conference. Conferences, circuits, and local churches were urged to organize mission societies and to seek funds for mission work. The United Brethren extended their missionary efforts into

northern New York, Canada, and the west. The Missionary Society of the Methodist Episcopal Church was established in 1820 by the General Conference. It was the successor to earlier unofficial missionary organizations. Its purpose was to raise funds for mission work and to keep the importance of missionary endeavor before the attention of the church. Missions on the frontier and in the cities, among Indians and blacks, were undertaken by various annual conferences and by the Missionary Society. The denomination's first "foreign" missionary projects included Liberia (1833) and South America (1835).

Publication

Publication was a fourth area of involvement. John Wesley had set an important example for Methodism by his own reading and study habits. He was convinced that Christians could mature by reading Christian literature, so he encouraged the printing and distribution of what he considered edifying material. American Methodism followed his lead. The Methodist Book Concern, which had been founded in 1789, was the first denominational publishing house in America. It continued to make available to Methodists and others a selection of carefully chosen books and tracts, many of which were from the pen of John Wesley. In the nineteenth century under the supervision of capable managers such as Joshua Soule, Nathan Bangs, and Beverly Waugh, the Book Concern not only offered an impressive list of books and pamphlets, but also succeeded in printing a theological journal for the denomination. It also published materials for women, children, youth, and the Sunday school. In 1826 it began publication of a weekly newspaper titled the *Christian Advocate,* which was most important for keeping the general membership informed. The printing operations and management of the Book Concern, originally located in

Philadelphia, were moved to New York City in 1804. A branch was subsequently opened in Cincinnati, and by midcentury a number of "depositories" were established in other cities. Book Concern profits were designated for the support of retired preachers and the widows and orphans of preachers.

The Evangelical Association contracted with private printers to publish materials as early as 1809. By 1816 the church purchased printing equipment and property to establish its own press in New Berlin, Pennsylvania. German-language hymnals, Disciplines, and other religious literature were produced for the membership. Not until 1832 did the church authorize an English Discipline and hymnbook. A newspaper for the general membership began publication in 1836. The United Brethren also worked with private printing businesses to produce materials, mostly hymnals and Disciplines, until the General Conference of 1833 authorized a "Printing Establishment." It was located at Circleville, Ohio. An official denominational newspaper was begun in 1834. Profits from the printing operations were designated for retired and "indigent" preachers and their families.

Democratic Crises and the Methodist Protestant Church

A number of church crises reflected the democratic mood that carried Andrew Jackson to the White House in 1828. For example, there was a dispute in the United Brethren Church between 1837 and 1841 concerning the role of the laity in amending the church's constitution. Methodism was ruptured by the founding of the Methodist Protestant Church in 1830.

During the first three decades of the nineteenth century, there was a strong concern in Methodism for broader participation by preachers and people in the life of the church.

A "reform" party surfaced in the 1820s that advocated three causes: the election of district superintendents rather than their appointment by the bishops; full conference membership for local preachers; and, most important of all, representation of the laity with the clergy in the policymaking conferences of the church. As a result of their agitation, some preachers and laypeople involved in the reform movement were either suspended or expelled from the church in 1827. Later that year they held a convention in Baltimore, the storm center of the dissent. The reformers pressed their cause again at the General Conference of 1828 but lost. Nevertheless, the movement continued to grow, and its leaders met again in Baltimore in November 1830 and organized the Methodist Protestant Church with an initial membership of 5,000. The new church's constitution eliminated the offices of bishop and district superintendent and secured lay representation from each circuit and station in annual conferences and equal ministerial and lay representation at the General Conference. Local preachers, however, did not gain annual conference membership.

II. Slavery, Division, and Civil War—1844 to 1865

Shortly after the American Revolution the number of voices raised against slavery began to increase. More Americans began to recognize the contradiction between the liberty for which the colonists had fought and the practice of slavery. Some argued that the dream of America as a Christian nation could never be realized so long as slavery existed among its people. Abolitionist sentiment grew slowly, often supported by the Second Great Awakening's concern for reform, and not without strong misgivings and vigorous opposition.

Until about 1830 a philosophy of gradual emancipation prevailed. But when William Lloyd Garrison founded the American Anti-Slavery Society in 1833 and demanded immediate freedom for the slaves, radical polarization of the nation began. While the abolitionist movement incurred opposition in both the North and the South, it became apparent by 1840 that slavery was evolving into a sectional issue that could threaten the nation's solidarity, as well as the unity of those Protestant churches with substantial memberships in both sections of the country. For example, the slavery question was a key factor in dividing Presbyterians and Baptists into northern and southern factions.

While the Evangelical Association and the United Brethren Church experienced some of the tensions created by the slavery problem, they did not suffer widespread divisiveness. Yet the fact that between 1841 and 1845 the United Brethren closed the pages of their denominational paper to the slavery controversy for fear that its circulation would be impaired indicates that their church was not entirely insulated from the dispute. Each of these denominations adopted a strong position against slavery. The 1816 General Conference of the Evangelical Assocation counseled its members to avoid the "buying and selling of men and women, whereby slavery is introduced or promoted." Their General Conference of 1839 prohibited the membership from owning or trading slaves. The third General Conference of the United Brethren, held in 1821, adopted the following legislation:

> Resolved and enacted, that no slavery, in whatever form it may exist, and in no sense of the word, shall be permitted or tolerated in our church; and should there be found any persons holding slaves, who are members among us, or make application to become such, then the former cannot remain, and the latter cannot become members of the United Brethren in Christ, unless they manumit their slaves as soon as they receive directions from the annual conference so to do. Neither shall any member of our church have the right to sell any of the slaves which he or she may now hold.

Methodists and Abolition

The Methodist Protestant Church and the Methodist Episcopal Church felt the full impact of the abolitionist quarrel; neither could avoid a formal sectional split after years of dispute. Since the Methodist Episcopal Church was a large and influential religious body in both the North and the South, it is probable that its division contributed to heightening the political disunity which finally divided the nation in 1861.

Methodism lived in the shadow of John Wesley's hatred

of slavery. He had condemned it in his tract, *Thoughts Upon Slavery*, published in 1774. He viewed slavery as "the sum of all villainies" and American slavery as "the vilest under the sun."

The slavery issue brewed in the Methodist Episcopal Church for several decades before it resulted in schism. Although antislavery agitation intensified at the 1836 and 1840 General Conferences, the church managed to avoid a breach. Many Methodists in the North and the South supported slavery for religious and biblical reasons as well as out of economic expediency. Some held that the question was purely political, unrelated to religion, and implored the church to remain aloof. The bishops feared that the issue would split the church. In 1836 they said that they had "come to the solemn conviction that the only safe, scriptural and prudent way for us, both as ministers and people to take, is wholly to refrain from the agitating subject."

Antislavery strength was gathering, however, particularly in the northern and western sections of the church. Orange Scott, a prominent ministerial member of the New England Conference and a vehement opponent of slavery, urged those with antislavery leanings to separate themselves from the Methodist Episcopal Church because it would not officially condemn the enslavement of human beings. In 1843 he organized the Wesleyan Methodist Church. His views probably accelerated antislavery activity among northern Methodists. The stage was set for decisive consideration of the problem.

The General Conference of 1844

The Methodist Episcopal General Conference of 1844 met in New York City. It was the longest ever held and recorded the largest number of roll call votes of any such meeting. There were two fundamental and interrelated issues with which it struggled: slavery and the relationship between the power of the General Conference and that of the bishops.

Two cases concerning slavery were presented to the delegates. The first involved an appeal by Francis Harding, a member of the Baltimore Annual Conference, who had been suspended for failing to free slaves acquired in marriage. The General Conference denied his appeal for reinstatement, a clear victory for the antislavery forces.

The second case involved Bishop James O. Andrew, one of the church's five episcopal leaders. Bishop Andrew had acquired two slaves, property of his first wife who bequeathed them to him upon her death. Furthermore, his second wife also owned slaves, although they remained her property and under her control. Andrew, therefore, rightly claimed that he had never bought or sold a slave. He stated that circumstances did not permit the emancipation of his family's slaves. Following lengthy debate, the General Conference approved a compromise resolution requiring Andrew to suspend the exercise of his episcopal duties as long as the slavery "impediment" remained. A minority report appeared protesting the action against Andrew. Soon a reply criticizing the protest was drafted and adopted.

Within a few days a Plan of Separation was presented to the delegates providing for annual conferences in slaveholding states to form their own distinct church if they desired. Local churches and conferences in the border states were free to choose by majority vote how they would align themselves if a new church were constituted. Clergy were given free choice in selecting which church they would join. There were also provisions concerning the distribution of property, especially that of the Book Concern.

While the slavery question appeared to be paramount at

the 1844 General Conference, another debate revolved around differing positions on church governance. The "conference" party, supported by a majority of the delegates, argued for a unilateral focus of power in the General Conference. It held that the bishops were only officers of the General Conference from which they derived whatever authority they possessed. The General Conference could discipline, as in the case of Bishop Andrew, and even expel, any bishop who was guilty of violating its dictates. The opposition, identified as the "constitutional" party, held that the constitution of the church placed the focus of power coordinately in the General Conference and the episcopacy and that, therefore, the disciplinary action against Bishop Andrew was unconstitutional.

Formation of the Methodist Episcopal Church, South

Within a year after the adoption of the Plan of Separation by the 1844 General Conference, delegates from annual conferences in the slaveholding states met in Louisville, Kentucky. They resolved to separate from the Methodist Episcopal Church and to create a new body called the Methodist Episcopal Church, South; at the same time a desire was expressed to maintain fraternal relations with the Methodist Episcopal Church. Arrangements were made to continue the publishing, educational, and mission work of the church. Bishops James O. Andrew and Joshua Soule were invited to be the episcopal leaders of the new body. The first General Conference of the new church was convened in Petersburg, Virginia, in 1846. A Discipline and a hymnbook were authorized at that meeting.

Reactions to the separation among the members of the Methodist Episcopal Church were mixed. While some found nothing objectionable about the course of events begun at the General Conference in 1844, others questioned the expediency and constitutionality of the Plan of Separation. In addition, there were numerous conflicts concerning the status of churches and annual conferences on the boundary between the two major sections of Methodism. The rivalry was intense between the two churches for the loyalty of Methodists living in the border states.

The 1848 General Conference of the northern church revealed hostility to the separation. Less than a third of the delegates to the 1844 General Conference were reelected. The 1848 meeting adopted a resolution not to enter into fraternal relations with the southern church and declared the Plan of Separation unconstitutional. Although the northern church could not force a reunion, since division was an accomplished fact, it could avenge the illegal breach by trying to withhold from the southern church an equitable distribution of the assets of the Book Concern. After lengthy litigation, however, the southern church was awarded by the Federal courts a share of the assets; and its 1854 General Conference selected Nashville, Tennessee, as the location of its publishing house.

Northern and Southern Methodists
Go Their Own Ways

The bitterness between the northern and southern churches continued into and beyond the 1850s. Each held general conferences, and each considered a variety of issues, some of which would change the life of Methodism long after the slavery question was put to rest. For example, the 1852 General Conference of the northern church considered petitions recommending lay representation in the annual and general conferences but retained by a vote of 171 to 3 the policy of no official voice for the laity.

Both churches discussed theological education. They endorsed the notion of an educated ministry, although theolog-

*L*ess *than a century after Americans adopted the slogan,
Join or Die, an attempt was made to disjoin the United
States. A political cartoon of the Civil War era shows President
Abraham Lincoln and Confederate President Jefferson Davis
tearing the nation's map. Nearly twenty years earlier, the
Methodist Episcopal Church was torn apart by the same
questions: slavery and divergent views of government.*

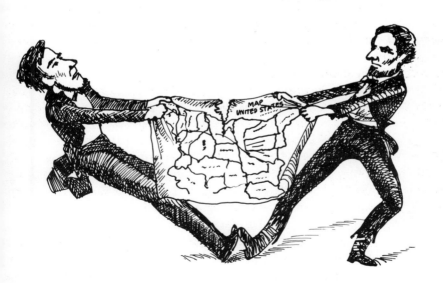

ical education was still a subject that stirred disagreement. There was much vocal opposition in the northern church, for example, when a Methodist Episcopal seminary was proposed for New York City. The belief persisted in some quarters that a formally educated ministry would be spiritually bankrupt and would produce a chasm between the clergy and the laity. Had they so easily forgotten that John Wesley's life testified to the unity of education and spirituality?

Slavery remained a major problem in both churches during the late 1850s. The northern church was besieged by petitioners who requested the church to exclude slaveholders from its membership. Others felt that exclusion was too radical. Nevertheless, abolitionist strength continued to swell among the Methodist Episcopal members. In the southern church the controversial provision of the General Rules that prohibited buying and selling slaves was finally removed in 1858. The southern church also adopted a philosophy affirming that it was not the business of the church to be involved with matters belonging to the jurisdiction of civil institutions. Slavery was a political issue, not a moral question. Therefore, it was better left in the hands of the government.

Lincoln's Election and Civil War

Abraham Lincoln was elected to the presidency of the United States in 1860. By the time of his inauguration in March 1861, the southern states had begun to secede and to form a new government, the Confederate States of America. Civil War began on April 12, 1861, when Confederates fired on Fort Sumter, South Carolina. The hostilities were to continue until Lee's surrender in 1865.

The northern and southern Methodist churches, which had become the largest and wealthiest Protestant bodies in their respective geographical areas, could not remain detached from the conflict. Tensions in the border conferences intensified. The bishops, religious press, and annual conferences of the northern church faithfully supported the Union cause. They engaged in patriotic demonstrations and recruited over five hundred chaplains for the Union Army. Valuable assistance was contributed to the United States Christian Commission, organized in 1861 to perform religious work among the troops. Methodist Episcopal clergy assisted with the enlistment of recruits. They followed the advancing Union Army into the South and tried to organize the work of the northern church, an action that bred a bitterness among southern Methodists that lasted for decades.

The southern church supported the Confederacy in a like manner. It authorized chaplains, distributed Bibles and religious literature, and conducted revivals among the troops. The clergy and religious press interpreted the war to countless southerners. Most of them were as convinced as those in the northern church that they were engaged in a fiery ordeal in which God's blessing rested on their side.

III. New Challenges—1866 to 1913

When the Civil War ended in 1865, the American people confronted a multitude of questions concerning the future of the nation. How would the former Confederate states be reintegrated into the Union? Could sectional antagonism be ameliorated? What would be the status of the four million freed slaves? How could the severely war-weakened southern economy be rehabilitated? These and other acute problems were dealt with in the program of Reconstruction. Next to the war itself, Reconstruction has often been judged as the most unpleasant chapter in nineteenth-century American life. Lasting into the late 1870s it was a period filled with revenge, animosity, deceit, and misunderstanding.

The Nation Begins to Change

Probably very few Americans in 1866 could foresee the difficulties of Reconstruction or the vast changes that would occur in their nation's life during the next half-century. Industrialization of the economy, led by the pronounced growth of heavy industry and the extension of the network of railroads, continued at a progressively increasing rate. Financial panics in 1873, 1893, and 1907 temporarily slowed economic growth and raised questions about the nation's economic philosophy. The expansion of industry gave birth to labor unrest and resulted in the organization of a powerful union movement. The population more than tripled its 1860 figure of 31 million. By 1915 it numbered more than 100 million. Approximately 20 million immigrants entered the country during this period. The size and number of cities indicated that the nation was becoming urbanized. These centers of population yielded their social and cultural blessings as well as the blight of poverty, exploitation, and corruption. The nation was influenced by intellectual developments such as Darwinism, the Chautauqua movement, and the strengthening of its public and private educational institutions. American churches were involved in the changes wrought by Reconstruction and the new challenges the succeeding decades presented.

One of the major concerns during Reconstruction was the rebuilding of the Methodist Episcopal Church, South. It had suffered with the rest of the Confederacy. The membership had fallen from 750,000 to less than 500,000. Its ministerial ranks were depleted. Many of the southern churches had been destroyed or seriously damaged; many had lost their leadership. The publishing, educational and mission activities had been suspended, and there was serious question about their restoration.

Some southern Methodists favored reunion with the northern church. But it was not to be. The Palmyra Manifesto of 1865, emanating from the Missouri Annual Conference, called for the continuation of the Methodist Episcopal Church, South. Furthermore, the southern bishops issued a Pastoral Address later in 1865 declaring loyalty to their church and calling for a General Conference in 1866. That meeting established the groundwork for rebuilding the publishing, educational, and mission programs. By 1870 it was clear that the southern church was recovering much of its prewar vitality.

Since the black membership of the southern church had

been rapidly eroding, the 1870 General Conference of the Methodist Episcopal Church, South, acted to form the Colored Methodist Episcopal Church, to which it intended to transfer all its remaining black members. A large number of its former black members had already been siphoned off by African Methodist Episcopal and African Methodist Episcopal Zion congregations instituted in the south. The Colored Methodist Episcopal Church was formally born in December 1870. William H. Miles and Richard H. Vanderhorst were elected its bishops and duly consecrated by Methodist Episcopal Church, South bishops. The denomination is known today as the Christian Methodist Episcopal Church.

The Churches Prosper

In spite of the difficulties of Reconstruction the postwar decades were prosperous for the churches that presently compose The United Methodist Church. There were significant increases in membership. From 1860 to 1920 the Methodist Church, South, grew from 750,000 to more than 2 million. The Methodist Episcopal Church increased from 1 million to well over 4 million. Membership in the Methodist Protestant Church grew from 60,000 to 185,000; the Evangelical Association from 40,000 to 240,000; and the United Brethren in Christ from 95,000 to 350,000. The number of congregations rose, and the churches became more affluent during the period. Between the Civil War and World War I, the churches rejoiced in their progress and endured the stresses that characterized the period.

Publishing, Education, and Worship

Still convinced that the printed page was a useful means for evangelizing, nurturing, and informing, the churches maintained their strong publishing programs. The publishing houses of the Evangelical Association and the United Brethren Church carried on their production of materials for the Sunday schools, the family, and the clergy. Their presses were busy printing a number of historical and theological works in addition to German- and English-language periodicals for the general membership. Financial difficulties, at times quite ominous, did not slow the three Methodist bodies from producing a steady stream of books, periodicals, and Sunday school literature. Their denominational newspapers and magazines helped to develop a solidarity among the members.

Building on their earlier involvement in Sunday schools and institutions of secondary and higher education, the churches were successful in enlarging their instructional ministries. All of them founded additional colleges and universities. They also sought to establish and implement higher educational standards for their clergy. Courses of study, the commonly accepted route of entry into the ministry, were made uniform across the churches and were regularly reexamined and improved. The need for a more thoroughly trained and formally educated ministry was increasingly acknowledged. By 1900 all the churches had opened at least one theological school for the professional education of their clergy. The seminaries were to play an increasingly critical role in the life of each church.

The Freedman's Aid Society deserves special mention as an important educational ministry developed after the Civil War. It was an agency of the Methodist Episcopal Church, sanctioned by the General Conference of 1868, with the primary purpose of establishing and maintaining educational institutions for freed slaves in the southern states. Among the schools started were Rust College, Holly Springs, Mississippi (1866), Clark College, Atlanta, Georgia (1869), Claflin College, Orangeburg, South Carolina (1869), and Meharry Medical College, Nashville, Tennessee (1876).

The post–Civil War period witnessed more formalized orders of worship in the churches. Elaborate organs, robed choirs, cushioned pews, and stained-glass windows helped to provide the setting. Hundreds of new churches were built each year, many in the Gothic revival and Romanesque architectural styles. Preachers could be identified by black suits, which were becoming standard clergy dress. Some preferred a Prince Albert coat, white vest, and white bow tie to conduct worship. Near the turn of the century some preachers wore a frock coat, winged collar, and striped trousers in the pulpit. Hymns, prayer, readings from scripture, and preaching remained the major components of worship. These were set within a more orderly liturgical structure than was generally the case earlier in the nineteenth century. Some clergy and laity felt that the newer formal worship did not permit as much freedom and spontaneity as they preferred. Others praised the solemnity and beauty of the more orderly arrangements. The Methodist Hymnal, jointly published in 1905 by the northern and southern Methodist churches, included a dignified order of service, tasteful music, and a psalter in the form of responsive readings. Preaching, however, continued to be worship's fundamental feature, and fresh, powerful sermons were highly regarded. Revised rituals for baptism and communion were provided and more widely used.

Theological and Structural Controversies

The era between the wars was marked by several theological and structural disagreements in the churches. Some of them were sufficiently grave to lead to schisms. One of the most disruptive debates involved the Wesleyan doctrine of holiness and sanctification. John Wesley had accentuated the importance of a holy life for Christians by stressing Christian perfection. Many Methodists interpreted Christian perfection in terms of a Christian's gradual maturing in God's grace and power. Others saw it as an instantaneous gift from God, a "second blessing," the "first blessing" being the sinner's conversion. American Methodism became polarized on the issue between 1870 and 1900.

A number of Methodists who favored the sudden "second blessing" approach and found precedent for it in Wesley's theology were instrumental in organizing a "holiness" movement among American Protestants. By means of their periodicals, camp meetings, and organizations, these holiness people were so centered on this interpretation of the gospel that they excited reaction and encountered strenuous opposition within Methodism. By the end of the century, convinced that Methodism could not be moved to correct its lack of holiness zeal, many of the proponents of the holiness position broke from the church and participated in the formation of a group of new churches such as the Church of the Nazarene and the Pilgrim Holiness Church. The Evangelical Association also bore the pain of discord on the matter of holiness and sanctification from 1848 to 1875. The issue was settled, however, without a major schism.

Other theological and structural questions troubled the churches. The United Brethren in Christ (Old Constitution) was formed by members of the United Brethren in Christ who objected to theological and constitutional legislation adopted at the General Conference of 1889. Discord among members of the Evangelical Association concerning the powers of bishops and a keen rivalry among the denomination's leaders led to a schism in 1894 when the United Evangelical Church was founded.

The rise of theological liberalism was also a source of quarrels in the churches. Darwin's theory of evolution was a central issue in these arguments, as was the scientific method of criticizing the Bible, which called into question old conclusions as to the authorship, chronology, and accuracy of the text of scripture. The liberal stress on the immanence and love of God rather than God's transcendence and judgment was debated. There was also much contention over the liberal emphasis on the humanity of Jesus to the exclusion of his deity.

Lay Participation

Long before the Civil War there was some sympathy for granting the laity a greater voice in determining the policies and actions of the churches. The Methodist Protestant Church had granted the laity official representation in its annual conferences and General Conference at the time of its formation in 1830. It was not until after the war, however, and not without decades of debate that the Methodist Episcopal Church, the Methodist Episcopal Church, South, the United Brethren, and the Evangelical Association granted laity an official voice in their affairs. The clergy were reluctant to concede the point, but by 1910 lay people had become voting delegates in the annual and general conferences. They were ultimately granted representation equal to that of the clergy. Lay membership in the conferences and in the growing host of church boards and agencies opened new opportunities at the national and regional levels for lay people to exercise the leadership they displayed in business and in their local congregations.

A struggle to involve women in the mainstream of the life of the churches was waged on at least two fronts. First, were women eligible for lay offices in the church and for the newly won lay representation in the conferences? An illustration of this issue was the 1888 General Conference of the Methodist Episcopal Church held in New York City. Five prominent women including Frances E. Willard, the famous leader of the Women's Christian Temperance Union, were properly elected delegates. Since women had never before been elected or seated as regular delegates at a General Conference, the question of their eligibility was raised. After spirited debate the conference decided that "laymen" meant men and refused to seat the women for constitutional, sociological, and theological reasons. The right of women to be regular delegates to a General Conference of the Methodist Episcopal Church was not finally resolved until 1904 when women were elected and admitted without question.

The second area of contention regarding the role of women concerned the question of their licensing and ordination as preachers. Women could serve the church as missionaries and deaconesses, but could they be licensed to preach and be ordained? Although women had applied for licenses to preach among the United Brethren early in the 1840s, the first woman to obtain permission was Charity Opheral in 1847. Four years later Lydia Sexton was regarded as "a Christian lady of useful gifts as a pulpit speaker" and was recommended as "a useful helper in the work of Christ." But not until 1889 did the United Brethren General Conference approve the ordination of women. By 1901 nearly a hundred women were listed in its ministerial directory.

The New York Conference of the Methodist Protestant Church ordained Anna Howard Shaw in 1880. Her ordination caused dissension within the denomination and was declared unlawful, but her annual conference recognized her orders. Ordination for women in the northern and southern Methodist churches was resisted. A major test case was brought before the Methodist Episcopal General Conference in 1880. Not only did the General Conference deny women the right of ordination, it also refused to license them as local preachers. Women were not granted full clergy right in

One or two women were recognized as potential preachers by the United Brethren in the 1840s, but women were not approved for ordination by that denomination until 1889. A Methodist Protestant woman was ordained in 1880. The Evangelical, Methodist Episcopal, and Methodist Episcopal, South churches never did grant women full clergy rights.

either church until after reunion in 1939. No women were ordained in the Evangelical Association.

Missionary Work

The five decades preceding the outbreak of World War I witnessed an explosive growth of Protestant missionary efforts. There was a renewed urgency to evangelize the unconverted and to recruit them for church membership. This fervor was two-dimensional. It emphasized home missions, including work among the unchurched in the cities, farmlands, and frontier. It also included foreign or overseas missions.

The churches supported and improved their missionary agencies. The Evangelical Association and the United Brethren had official denominational boards that promoted their work at home and in such distant locales as Africa, Germany, China, Japan, and the Philippines. Each had active women's organizations, which upheld the work with personnel, funds, and educational programs.

The northern and southern Methodists carried on effective mission work among the American Indians. They often competed keenly with each other as they expanded and strengthened their work in such territories as Colorado, Montana, Wyoming, Oregon, and California. They had begun work in China, India, and Europe before the Civil War. They enlarged their efforts in those areas and added other missions in Asia, Africa, and Latin America. The Methodist Protestant Church also sponsored home and foreign work. The latter was largely confined to Japan before World War I.

Women were leaders in the missionary movement. Through their offerings, educational and recruitment endeavors, and their own enlistment to serve on the mission field, women contributed invaluable assistance to the missionary crusade. The Woman's Foreign Missionary Society of the Methodist Episcopal Church was born in 1869. Eleven years later Methodist Episcopal women formed the Woman's Home Missionary Society. Similar groups were formed by Methodist Episcopal Church, South, and Methodist Protestant women. The United Brethren and Evangelical Association women also had mission societies prior to 1900.

Important mission work centered on the needs of immigrant and ethnic groups in America. The Evangelical Association and the United Brethren in Christ, with their predominantly German cultural and language origins, had a natural advantage in attracting the German immigrant population. The Methodists developed work among the Germans largely due to the leadership of William Nast, a well-educated German immigrant, converted in 1835. Nast was instrumental in organizing the first German Methodist society in America in 1838. Methodist home mission work was also begun among the Scandinavians, Japanese, Chinese, Italians, Cubans, Mexicans, and Indians. Some of this activity became sufficiently large to be organized into ethnic annual conferences. The rest was preserved in bilingual missions.

Two important facts must be noted at this point. First, the Methodist work among the various language groups in America supplied the impetus for missions to Germany and the Scandinavian countries. Methodist churches were founded in those European nations as a result of the affiliations of many of their sons and daughters in America. Second, the ministries to immigrants were not without the tensions created by a periodically resurgent American nativism that resented the economic, political, and cultural threats posed by the newcomers. The churches sometimes found themselves strained between a commitment to assist the recently arrived in spiritual and material ways and a wish that they had stayed in their native lands. In this matter the churches reflected the ambivalence of the larger society.

Social Problems

American Protestants responded to late nineteenth-century social problems in at least two ways. Some believed that the best solution was traditional revivalism as updated by Dwight L. Moody and other evangelists—convert the individual, and ultimately society would be reformed. Others insisted that economic, political, and social problems were more than individual issues and, therefore, that society's institutions must be reformed. A movement known as social Christianity or the Social Gospel emerged from the latter group. Although it was quite diverse, the movement was one of the most important Protestant ventures between the wars.

The churches whose histories we are investigating supported both the revivalistic and Social Gospel crusades. Since the two philosophies of dealing with social problems were often incompatible, it is not surprising that there were conflicts in the churches between the proponents of each. Nevertheless, the churches recognized the necessity of speaking to, and acting upon, the social problems plaguing the nation.

Alcoholic beverages were identified as a major cause of social and individual decay. Therefore, the churches actively promoted total abstinence. The Methodists, the Evangelical Association, and the United Brethren each had a history of opposition to alcohol going back to the antebellum period. After the war they became very active in the campaign to outlaw alcoholic beverages. Moral suasion and political action were utilized to achieve the goal of total abstinence. One of the extraordinary national figures in the crusade against alcohol was Frances E. Willard, a member of the Methodist Episcopal Church, who was also an ardent proponent of women's rights.

The churches underscored their disdain for the con-

*T*he plight of workers concerned many Christians during the closing years of the nineteenth century, although they were divided in their attitudes toward unions and strikes. By 1908, however, the Methodist Episcopal Church was ready to favor unions, improvement of working conditions, equitable wages, and protection for women and children in the work force.

sumption of alcoholic beverages by using grape juice in their communion services. In the Methodist Episcopal Church, for example, grape juice was recommended by the General Conference of 1864. By 1880 it was required "whenever practicable," but not until 1916 was it made mandatory without qualification.

The plight of workers was one of the principal concerns of the Social Gospel. While many church leaders and members opposed unionization and strikes, there were a few who spoke in behalf of the workers. Because the Methodist Episcopal Church and the Methodist Episcopal Church, South, were often controlled by middle-class attitudes, they sometimes appeared indifferent to the conditions of the working class. Yet the Methodist Federation for Social Service, founded in 1907, and the Social Creed, legislated by the 1908 General Conference, prove that the northern church was not oblivious to the situation of the worker. The creed called for "equal rights and complete justice for all men in all stations of life." It favored labor unions, improvement of working conditions, a living and equitable wage, and protection for women and children in the work force. The Methodist Social Creed served as a pattern for the social concerns document of the Federal Council of Churches.

Interchurch Cooperation

Despite occasional schismatic developments in the late nineteenth and early twentieth centuries, there were important developments in interchurch cooperation and even negotiations for union. The United Brethren were involved in conversations with the Methodist Protestant and the Congregational churches for several years after the turn of the century. Both the Evangelical Association and the Methodist Episcopal Church discussed union between 1859 and 1871. When negotiations failed to materialize, the Evangelical

Association strengthened its ties and fellowship with the United Brethren.

Efforts were made to improve the relationship between the Methodist Episcopal Church and the Methodist Episcopal Church, South. Delegations from both churches met in Cape May, New Jersey, in 1876 to discuss their mutual ties and to affirm a strong sense of fraternity. Although reunion would not occur for more than sixty years the groundwork was laid for the conversations and actions that would bring it to pass.

The Ecumenical Methodist Conferences held in 1881, 1891, 1901, and 1911 were another means by which churches of the world-wide Methodist family gathered to discuss their home and foreign work, to promote cooperation, and to increase their common moral and evangelical power.

Not only did the spirit of cooperation flourish among the five forerunners of United Methodism, they also became parties to the larger ecumenical movement that began to flower during the decades preceding World War I. Each of them joined the Federal Council of Churches, the first major ecumenical venture among American Protestants. Its purpose was to "express the fellowship and catholic unity of the Christian Church" and to "secure a larger combined influence for the churches of Christ in all matters affecting the moral and social condition of the people, so as to promote the application of the law of Christ in every relation of human life."

Whither?

Nearly a century after the deaths of Albright, Boehm, Otterbein, and Asbury, the churches they started could rejoice in their growth and bask in a feeling of optimism about the future. This sense of confidence was compounded of the

Christian doctrine that God works in all things for good and the secular doctrine that things are getting better and better all the time. But before long the secular doctrine of progress would suffocate in the trenches in France, and the churches would find their trust in God's providence challenged by war, economic crises, racism, new moralities, sexism, and theological change.

Part Three

The Twentieth Century

by Kenneth E. Rowe

*T*wentieth-century worship in the churches of United Methodism has reappropriated the ancient tradition of ordered Christian worship — a tradition native to United Methodists through their Anglican, Lutheran, and Reformed roots, but a heritage largely neglected in the nineteenth century. Churches are now designed to be symbolic as well as functional, the Christian year has been rediscovered, candles join the cross on communion tables, robed choirs process down center aisles, and pastors appear in colored vestments.

I. Maturity and Status in the New Century—1914 to 1939

The shock of World War I brought the nineteenth century to an irrevocable close. A new world, distressed by war, depression, and what appeared to be moral chaos, emerged in its aftermath. But it was also a world of promise, blessed with light bulbs and indoor plumbing, telephones and movies, radios and refrigerators, automobiles for new-style circuit riders, and that pearl of great price for the churches, the mimeograph machine!

Maturity and status were at last marks of the three families of churches. Small rural churches, large ones on a thousand main streets, and great cathedral-style buildings in the cities comfortably housed the people called Evangelicals, United Brethren, and Methodists on Sunday mornings. Dominantly middle class, the three churches also included the very poor and the very privileged. They were led by an increasing corps of seminary-trained pastors and able bishops and were challenged by ambitious programs set forth by a growing number of churchwide boards and agencies. Optimistic about the prospects for a better age and confident that they had a large role to play in bringing it about, a half-million Evangelicals and United Brethren and five million Methodists were mobilized for mission.

Piety, Patriotism, and Prohibition

The early part of the twentieth century saw a new interest in peace. It was the height of respectability to condemn war as barbaric. Many believed world peace through arbitration was just around the corner. Methodists, Evangelicals, and the United Brethren at their general conferences between 1912 and 1916 supported these ideals.

America's entry into the war in 1917 ended all that for the time being. Although a few continued to support pacifist ideals, the coming of war brought forth a crude mixture of idealism and crass nationalism, a holy crusade for democracy abroad and a stifling of freedom at home.

Evangelicals celebrated their founder Jacob Albright as a Revolutionary War hero and urged his latter-day flock to follow his example as patriot. The Methodist press openly attacked Quakers and other pacifists. Some Evangelical, United Brethren, and German Methodist congregations had the cornerstones of their churches painted yellow, their pastors threatened, and members insulted as un-American. These actions must be seen in the context of the patriotic fever in the country generally. Methodists, Evangelicals, and United Brethren were no more and no less involved than other churches. They were simply reflecting the predominant mood of the times. Yet the churches did not yield completely to the national mood. The United Brethren General Conference of 1917, noting that "a vein of pure German blood runs through our whole church from Otterbein to the present," passed a resolution requesting "our people everywhere to refrain from any unkind criticism of their German brethren in this country." A few Methodist annual conferences went on record opposing patriotic excesses.

In the years that followed the Treaty of Versailles, revulsion against *world* war gave rise to a new wave of pacifism. Methodists, Evangelicals, and United Brethren adopted

*A*merica's entry into World War I in 1917 ended
the passion for peace previously exhibited by Evangelicals,
Methodists, and United Brethren. The churches cooperated with
the government in what President Woodrow Wilson called a
crusade to make the world safe for democracy. Quakers and
other pacifists were attacked by the Methodist press.

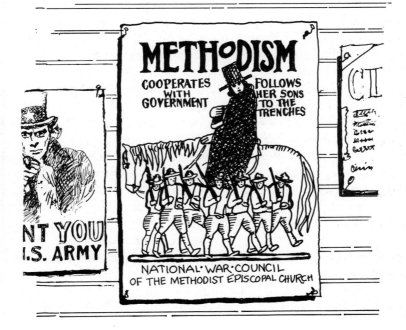

resolutions on peace and became active in peace societies until another world war loomed on the horizon to test their commitment.

In the first half of the twentieth century the emphasis upon personal morality among the Methodists, Evangelicals, and United Brethren was not relaxed. This concern found clearest expression in the churches' advocacy of total abstinence from alcoholic beverages. All three churches had been working on this front for almost a century. Temperance societies had long been recommended in all congregations and Sunday schools; Temperance Sunday with its pledge became an annual event; grape juice had been ordered for communion services since the 1880s; temperance literature of all kinds was penned, published, and promoted. By the declaration of several general conferences early in the twentieth century, the churches announced their intention to achieve moral reform through the agency of the state. During the period between the enactment of Prohibition in 1920 and its repeal in 1933, their primary public interest was to defend Prohibition.

The presidential election of 1928 brought the matter to political focus with the nomination of a Roman Catholic candidate. The prime reason Methodists, Evangelicals, and United Brethren opposed Al Smith was not because he was Catholic, but because he was "wet." The battle was won in 1928, but the war was lost in 1933 when Prohibition was repealed. Although sobriety by law appears to be a thing of the past, United Methodists continue to struggle against alcoholism and its consequences.

Mutations Within the Connectional System
In the United Methodist understanding of the church, there has been a long-standing tension between the initial emphasis on small voluntary religious societies within "established" churches — the Methodists within the Church of En-

gland, Evangelicals and United Brethren within Lutheran and Reformed churches—and the emphasis that has developed over the course of two centuries on being a distinctive denomination. These twin concepts of religious society and institutional church with their respective values and concerns have never been wholly reconciled. On the one hand, the basic premise of the small group is the principle of subsidiary and local initiative. It is in the local communities, and the small groups within them, that the Holy Spirit nurtures meaningful experiences, which then seek wider avenues of mission and outreach. On the other hand, United Methodists, believing themselves led by the same Spirit, have a long tradition of connectional administration by conferences, bishops, and program boards and of developing every aspect of a full-fledged institutional church.

Throughout the nineteenth century power in the several churches lay principally in the hands of the bishops and conferences. By the turn of the century, however, with big business and big government on the horizon, Evangelicals, United Brethren, and Methodists alike began to develop bureaucracy on a grand scale. The development had its beginnings with the formation of publishing houses and missionary societies in the nineteenth century, but it was not until the present century that these publishing and mission boards, plus a whole family of new ones, began to compete with bishops and conferences for power and influence in the church. Increasingly it was the staffs of these boards who began to shape the policy and program of the church, which then was approved by the conferences and promoted by the bishops and district superintendents.

Fading Force of Ethnic Diversity/ Modest Gains for Women

Although the heavy flow of immigration to America was greatly reduced in the early decades of this century, this did not mean the immediate end of foreign-language services, hymnbooks, Disciplines, and a cluster of ethnic annual conferences. One-third of the population in 1920 was still foreign born. In that year ten German, six Swedish, and two Norwegian-Danish annual conferences were flourishing in the Methodist Episcopal Church. Twenty years later, however, all of them had disappeared. The United Brethren quietly discontinued work in the German language in 1933. The use of German among the Evangelicals was given up in 1922. In every case the time came when the younger members, impatient with the old ways, sought modernization and Americanization and campaigned for the English language. The same thing happened to the family of Asian Methodists on the west coast, but much more slowly. In this period only the Spanish-speaking Methodists preserved and strengthened their cultural identity.

Inspired by their success in gaining the right to vote in 1920, women revived their struggle for rights within their churches. Unlike the United Brethren who, with the Methodist Protestants, led the way by granting laity and clergy rights to women in the 1880s, Methodists and Evangelicals had resisted the trend. A major victory for laity rights for women had been won in the northern Methodist General Conference of 1900, but the Methodist Episcopal Church, South, moved more slowly in giving rights to women. As late as 1914, there was heated debate in the southern General Conference on the right of women to be elected stewards in local churches and to hold other representative positions in the church. In 1918 the General Conference finally approved laity rights for women by a large majority.

Nevertheless, only half the battle had been won. Methodist women, south and north, were now full-fledged "laymen"—but could they be full-fledged clergy also? The 1920 General Conference of the Methodist Episcopal

Church took the first step by granting women local preacher's licenses. Four years later Methodist women launched another offensive. The 1924 General Conference, sensing the indifference of the church at large to the matter of the ordination of women, saw no need to recommend change. Yet there was one small breakthrough. Recognizing the "very evident and acute need for an effective sacramental ministry on the part of women in certain home and particularly the foreign fields," the conference approved the ordination of women as local preachers. Through these same years the Evangelical Church and the southern Methodists remained aloof from the whole movement.

Loosening Ties to the Theological Tradition

There were clear signs in the 1890s that a theological shift was in the wind. "Liberal" Protestantism, a movement to modernize theology that had been developing for decades, caught up with Evangelicals and United Brethren as well as Methodists. But until 1930 the older patterns of evangelical theology inherited from the previous century were still dominant.

A bitter battle raged between conservatives and liberals (Fundamentalists and Modernists, to use their labels) in the 1920s. Conservatives saw the liberals as subversives of the faith; liberals saw themselves as saviors of the essence of the faith. By the end of the decade the conservatives lost control and the liberals were in command, first in the seminaries and then afterward in the church generally—on the episcopal bench, in the boards and agencies, behind the editorial desks, and in the pulpits and Sunday school classrooms across the land.

Traces of traditional evangelicalism—the centrality of Jesus Christ, the stress on personal salvation, and the longing for God's kingdom—continued, but each with a new twist.

Convinced that to know the good is to do it, liberals preferred to talk about Christ as teacher rather than Christ as Redeemer. Confident that gradualism was the normal pattern of Christian growth, liberals abandoned the older pattern of sudden conversion. Certain that evangelical otherworldliness needed to be traded for a focus on this world, liberals located God's kingdom more and more in this world and made building the kingdom more and more a human responsibility. This led to the most crucial change of all, as far as the legacy from Wesley, Otterbein, and Albright is concerned. Liberals tended to displace the older optimism of grace, based on what God does in us through the Holy Spirit, with a new optimism of nature, based on what we do on our own apart from God.

The reigning liberal theology of the time called for changes in the rituals of all but the Evangelicals, whose form of worship had a minimum of ritual. The United Brethren revised their rituals in 1921, and the new hymnal of 1935 contained more elaborate worship resources. The southern Methodists remained the most conservative and made only minor changes in the services derived from Wesley's prayer book. Northern Methodists were less reluctant to change: minor changes occurred in 1916; major changes in 1932. A new Methodist hymnal, jointly produced by the Methodists north and south and the Methodist Protestants in 1935, contained four orders for Sunday worship, including a modest revision of Wesley's formal order for Morning Prayer. The trend was heavily in the direction of dignified order, both in liturgy and music. Only the black Methodist churches retained the spontaneity, rhythmic music, and high degree of participation characteristic of nineteenth-century worship patterns.

Church architecture and worship habits reflected the

times. The trend everywhere was toward more formal structures. By the 1920s the churches were in the midst of a
Gothic revival. Victorian churches built on the Akron
plan—semi-circular sanctuaries with curved pews on sloping
floors and central pulpits and choir lofts behind—gave way
to pseudo-Gothic "cathedrals," complete with divided
chancels and elaborate altars. Choral music came to be a normal part of worship, often at the expense of congregational
singing. The Christian year was rediscovered, along with liturgical colors, candles joined the cross on countless communion tables, robed choirs processed down center aisles, and
ministers appeared in pulpit gowns instead of cutaways. The
once popular midweekly prayer meeting fell victim to Edgar
Bergen and Charlie McCarthy, Fibber McGee and Molly,
and the Lux Radio Theater.

In this period standards of preaching also changed. Moving away from the style of the free evangelists who were
now frowned upon, sermons were better structured and full
of literary allusions, testimony to the "higher standards" set
by seminary preaching courses. These changes in worship
style reflected profound changes in the worshipers.

The Rocky Roads to Reunion:
Evangelicals in 1922, Methodists in 1939

As the Methodist, Evangelical, and United Brethren
churches grew, they also divided. During the early decades
of this century, however, Evangelicals and Methodists
wound their way down what turned out to be rocky roads
to reunion. Both churches found rocks in the way—mostly
personalities for the Evangelicals; the presence of a large
number of blacks in the northern church for the Methodists.
Both divisions were sectional in nature—east versus west for
the Evangelicals; north versus south for the Methodists.

For many years rivalry simmered between two factions of the Evangelical Association. The western Indianapolis-based majority favored German language, strong bishops, and a conservative theological stance; the eastern Philadelphia-based minority favored English, a curtailed episcopacy and openness to new theological developments. In 1891 there was a split that was not healed until 1922. The newly united church was christened the Evangelical *Church*.

Black slavery and the white racism that supported it were among the causes of Methodist divisions. By the turn of the century great difficulties arose from the presence of two families of white Methodist churches in the South. In-fighting, especially bitter in the border states, caused the two churches to seek a resolution of their differences. Other influences were at work toward the reunification of Methodists north and south—fraternal delegates appeared at each other's general conferences; rivalries were adjusted on the foreign mission field; both churches actively supported the work of emerging ecumenical bodies such as the Federal Council of Churches. The two churches even began to sing and pray alike, since they produced common hymnals and rituals in 1905 and again in 1935. As a result of these and other factors, Methodists north and south, early in this century began to wind their way down the rocky road to reunion.

Throughout all these years of talking union the one constant rock making the road rough was the presence of a significant number of blacks in the northern Methodist church. In 1916, the year when union talks began in earnest, the southern church had no black members, while the northern church had more than a quarter of a million. Was it possible to devise a basis for union that would not offend southern sensibilities and yet would adhere to the north's historic mission to the blacks?

*T*he twentieth century has witnessed a number of church reunions. Two Evangelical factions formed the Evangelical Church in 1922. Three Methodist churches—Methodist Episcopal, Methodist Protestant, and Methodist Episcopal, South—came together in The Methodist Church in 1939. The Church of the United Brethren in Christ and the Evangelical Church created the Evangelical United Brethren Church in 1946. At a uniting conference held in Dallas, Texas, in 1968, the Methodist and Evangelical United Brethren churches became The United Methodist Church.

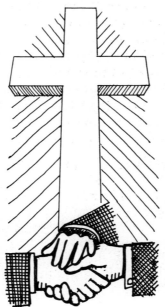

Differing approaches to the office of bishop, the authority of the General Conference, the idea of jurisdictions, and especially the status of black ministers and members led to the failure of a preliminary plan of union in 1924. The South talked of "absorption," the North of "excessive regionalism." Hopes for a speedy reunion were dashed until the end of the decade when several Methodist Protestant leaders proposed a fresh start on a three-way union. Teams of negotiators were authorized at the three churches' next general conferences. The joint commission began to work at once and by 1935 had hammered out a plan of union, the most controversial feature of which was the proposed jurisdictional structure of the new church. The country was to be divided into six administrative units—five by geography and one by race.

To be adopted, the plan of union had to receive constitutional majorities from the general and annual conferences of the uniting churches. The plan's first test came at the General Conference of the Methodist Protestant Church in May 1936, where it was approved by a wide margin after modest debate. Large-scale debate occurred at the General Conference of the Methodist Episcopal Church later that month. Whether segregation was being legislated into the church or not was the key issue. Supporters of the plan said it was not. They argued that it was nothing more than the continuation of the policy of the northern church since the Civil War. Critics replied that whatever had happened in the past was past. They pointed out that although the church had been living with segregated annual conferences for almost a century, this was the moment to change the pattern, not to imbed it deeper into the church's life and constitution. Drafters of the plan claimed the intent behind the all-black Central Jurisdiction was not segregationist, but an arrangement to protect the black minority in the new church, since each jurisdiction elected its own bishops and had equal representation on the general program boards of the church.

Black delegates at the General Conference voted over-whelmingly against the plan; white delegates approved it by a wide margin. After the Methodist Episcopal General Conference ratified the plan, it was sent down to the annual conferences. Black annual conferences rejected the plan; however the church as a whole sustained it. It was only as the black vote began to come in that some church people began to question the morality of pushing blacks into an arrangement they obviously didn't want.

During this time the southern church was not unattentive to the history that was being made north of the Mason-Dixon Line. Silence on the matter of the plan of union was broken only as it became clear that the North was going to endorse it. While there was considerable support for reunion in the South, there was little enthusiasm for a united church with black ministers and members, even if set apart in segregated structures. But in the end, at their General Conference of 1938, the Methodist Episcopal Church, South, approved the plan. The Central Jurisdiction was the price for which, by moral compromise, the union of Methodists north and south was purchased.

II. Programmed Churches and Social Ferment—1939 to 1968

Throughout the decade of the 1930s there was a good deal of somber anxiety—banks failed, dictators prowled, wars raged abroad. Yet there were also moments of excitement and drama—abroad a king abdicated (and all for love!), at home we had marathon dancing, alphabet soup, and license once more to drink to it all. The most exciting moment for the Methodists came in the spring of 1939 in Kansas City, Missouri. The three major branches of American Methodism at last united. Seven years later the Evangelical Church and the United Brethren Church joined to form the Evangelical United Brethren Church. A plan of union had been accepted by wide margins by the general conferences of the Evangelical Church in 1942 and the United Brethren Church in 1945. Following the required approval, a uniting conference was held in the First United Brethren Church in Johnstown, Pennsylvania, in November 1946, to announce the birth of the new church. Together the two new churches included eight and a half million members; their households made the community still larger.

Pacifism and Participation: World War II

As in World War I so in World War II, there was a coalescence of piety and patriotism. Total war meant that the country fought with a moral passion that made her patriotism almost indistinguishable from her piety. By the eve of the war Methodists, Evangelicals, and United Brethren had developed strong peace positions. The uniting conference of the Methodists in 1939 adopted a resolution "in opposition to the spirit of war now raging through the world." The spring of 1941 brought the nation and the churches one step closer to war, but the United Brethren General Conference continued to press for peace. Although making no attempt to bind the consciences of its individual members, the conference pledged itself not to endorse, support, or participate in war. Those who were conscientious objectors were promised the support of the church.

Within a few months after the conference adjourned the nation was at war; the positions for peace of the several churches would meet their toughest tests. Less than a year after Pearl Harbor, the Evangelical Church gathered for its General Conference and reaffirmed its prewar position that "war and bloodshed are not agreeable to the Gospel of Jesus Christ," recognized the status of conscientious objectors, and approved the office and ministry of military chaplains, but added that such action was "not to be construed as implying the endorsement of war by our church."

The second General Conference of the Methodist Church met two and a half years after the nation was officially at war. Could the Methodists in 1944 maintain their prewar stand as the Evangelicals had done? A report prepared by Ernest F. Tittle reaffirmed the pacifist position of 1939; a substitute written by Charles C. Parlin blessed the soldiers, prayed for victory, and called for an all-out war effort. The clergy voted 170 to 169 in favor of the Parlin position, while the laity supported it 203 to 131 — clear evidence of the long way that Methodism had come in the years since World War I. The troubled conscience of Methodism on matters of war and peace was shared by the United Brethren, who met for their last General Conference during the closing year of the war.

As the war dragged on, Methodists, Evangelicals, and United Brethren alike developed a sustaining conviction about the need for a responsible world political organization. A "Crusade for a New World Order" initiated by Methodist Bishop G. Bromley Oxnam in 1943 was a model educational and action campaign envisioning plans for the postwar world. Dialogue between bishops and political leaders in Washington was crucial to both sides. When American Protestantism in 1945 rallied behind the United Nations conference in San Francisco, the moral and political voice of the United States, in part at least, had been shaped by Methodism's crusade.

Programming Mission/Eliminating Racism and Sexism

With the formation of the Methodist and Evangelical United Brethren churches, there were continuing changes in polity and practice. The program boards proliferated and gained power and influence. Formal recognition was given to them in 1939 when the Methodists created the Council of Secretaries to balance the Council of Bishops. Programs developed by the boards were adopted by the general and annual conferences and passed on to the people by bishops, superintendents, and clergy. Following two "successful" crusades (1944–1953) the idea of a quadrennial emphasis was written into the law of the Methodist Church in 1952, and a new board was created to promote future crusades—the Commission on Promotion and Cultivation. The "United Crusade" of the Evangelical United Brethren Church, 1954–1958, which brought in five million dollars, was an example of the new church's program in action.

Racism

Methodists have long been involved in a continuing struggle to eliminate racial barriers inside and outside the church. Successive general conferences since 1939 received increasing numbers of petitions for legislation on the issue symbolized by the all-black Central Jurisdiction.

Momentum to abolish the Central Jurisdiction increased in the early 1950s, influenced by the attention given to the Supreme Court's school desegregation decision of 1954. The first concrete step came at the 1956 General Conference, where there were more than four thousand petitions on the race issue alone. The conference passed a forthright resolution condemning "racial discrimination or enforced segregation," established a churchwide quadrennial program on race and, most important of all, adopted legislation that would permit the transfer of black local churches and annual conferences into the white jurisdictions in which they were situated.

In the next eight years only a few annual conferences and local churches transferred. By 1964 there were still seventeen black annual conferences. Pressure was building on both sides. Should the church enforce its resolution on race within its fellowship or wait until each area of the country saw fit to take action? After a long and bitter debate the General Conference of 1964 adopted a two-step plan to abolish the Central Jurisdiction. A deadline of September 1967 was set to transfer all black annual conferences into regional jurisdictions. Merging annual conferences within their new jurisdictions became a mandate. Within a year all the black annual conferences had merged except those in the South. A special session of the General Conference in 1966 postponed the deadline.

In the meantime, union negotiations were coming to a head with the Evangelical United Brethren, who had a long history of strong antislavery sentiment and action. The plan that created The United Methodist Church in 1968 eliminated the Central Jurisdiction by failing to mention a jurisdiction based on race, but separate black annual conferences continued on into the early 1970s. United Methodism's conscience was still troubled.

Sexism

In the Methodist Church the issue of full clergy rights for women came up regularly at each successive General Conference. There was a flurry of excitement in the late 1930s when the plan of union was being drafted that the new church would grant such rights to its women, especially since women already had such rights in the Methodist Protestant Church. The uniting conference in 1939 failed by a close vote to grant full clergy rights to women. Methodist women continued to press the issue at successive General Conferences. The struggle for full clergy rights was finally won in 1956. The number of women ministers, however, did not swell. Not till the late 1970s did women in increasing numbers test the commitment of the church.

While Methodist women gained a major victory in 1956, United Brethren women were handed a severe setback at the time of union with the Evangelicals in 1946. Although the United Brethren granted full clergy rights to women as early as 1889, and had a long tradition of women in their seminaries and in their pulpits, they agreed to follow the example of the Evangelical Church and give up the practice.

Ecumenism Family-Style

In the last century the word "ecumenical" signified the worldwide family of Methodist churches. But a Methodist layman changed all that in the early decades of this century. He was John R. Mott, the one man above all others who gave impetus and organized direction to the ecumenical movement of the twentieth century. For this he was awarded the Nobel Peace Prize. His living monument is the World Council of Churches.

Since 1900 few councils of churches or ecumenical projects have been without Evangelical, Methodist, and United Brethren participation. But by midcentury the churches were caught up in the tension of opposing forces — one pushing them toward cooperation if not union; the other pulling them back from unreserved ecumenical commitment and possible surrender of precious traditions and institutions. This matter came to a head in the mid-1960s when the churches seemed to be heading in two directions at once. Both churches were members of the Consultation on Church Union (COCU) in the United States in which nine American Protestant churches sought some form of visible church unity. At the same time the World Methodist Council, which was formed in 1951 as a continuing secretariat between World Methodist Conferences, was pushing for the Methodists of the world to unite. The issue boiled down to open versus closed ecumenism. Failing to make a clear choice, ecumenical energies were focused instead on expediting the Methodist–Evangelical United Brethren merger.

A scant ten years after the formation of the Evangelical United Brethren Church, it began to wind its way down the relatively smooth road to union with the Methodists. Formal discussions began in 1956. Ten years later a plan of union had been readied for consideration by the two churches meeting simultaneously in General Conference in Chicago. The constitution and proposed Book of Discipline favored the Methodist pattern on all important points of difference. As the conferences began to vote, it was clear that the delegates representing the two churches were very different in their attitude to union. Evangelical United Brethren delegates squeezed past the adequate number by a mere 15 votes! The Methodists voted in favor of the plan by a huge majority. The next year the respective annual conferences of the two churches ratified the plan with sufficient majorities. The United Methodist Church was about to be born!

III. Merger and Reappraisal at Midcentury—1968 to 1984

Lord of the Church
We are united in Thee
in Thy Church
And now in The United Methodist Church!

With these words Evangelical United Brethren Bishop Reuben H. Mueller and Methodist Bishop Lloyd C. Wicke announced the formation of The United Methodist Church to the uniting conference in Dallas, Texas, on April 23, 1968. That beginning, inspiring as it was, appears in retrospect more a grand pageant marking the merger of two similar bodies than the creation of something distinctively new. The high moment of spiritual exultation at the uniting conference was immediately followed by three quadrennia of dealing with an accumulation of issues the drafters of the plan of union preferred to postpone. Part of the dilemma was the social trauma that was Vietnam.

The United Methodist Church was born at a time when Americans were more divided than they had been for generations. The nation was in the midst of its longest and most troubling war. President Johnson's dramatic escalation of the war in 1965 sparked fierce debate. Some church people urged young men to resist the draft; others believed they had an obligation to serve their country in the armed forces. The

morality of war troubled the consciences of United Methodists during this period and threatened to divide them once
again. In the spring of 1972, when North Vietnam launched
a major offensive with sharp gains in the south, President
Nixon reacted by intensifying American bombing. Within
weeks, United Methodists gathered for their first General
Conference. Following a long debate the conference adopted
a statement condemning the "immorality" of America's involvement in the war and called on President Nixon to halt
the bombing. Within one year a ceasefire was arranged,
but the anger between pro- and antiwar church members
remained.

Postponed Union Homework: Growing-Together Pains

The ruling principle of the commission that worked out
the 1968 Methodist–Evangelical United Brethren merger
was unite now, settle the differences later. Issues such as
ministry and episcopacy, doctrinal standards and social principles, the number of seminaries and an unbelievably com-
plicated cluster of national program boards were not addressed. The uniting conference established a pattern of
churchwide quadrennial study commissions to tackle them
one by one.

The study attracting most attention during the first
quadrennium and at the 1972 General Conference was the
report of the Structure Study Commission. There was widespread hope of the possibility of reversing the century-old
trend of "one board after another" and even paring down the
church's bureaucracy. In the end the boards and agencies
were merely grouped into four super boards–Church and
Society, Discipleship, Global Ministries, and Higher Education and Ministry. A simplified one-word description of each
respectively is–advocacy, nurture, outreach, and vocation.

The quota system for electing members created new and uncertain boards, but youth, women, and ethnic minority representatives gained a voice, while white middle-aged males learned the consequences of sharing authority.

United Methodism, like any organized structure, bewails overlapping, duplication, and waste. The former Methodist Church had established a Coordinating Council to get the boards to work together, but the council was never really effective. In the former Evangelical United Brethren Church, coordination was far more effective through a national Council on Ministries. In the united church the Evangelical United Brethren structure was adopted, but debate continues on its effectiveness.

The 1972 General Conference continued the postponed union homework by establishing three study commissions of its own—one to study the seminaries, another to study ministry and ordination, and a third to study episcopacy and superintendency. Four years later the reports came in. The general church accepted major responsibility for funding ministerial education and reduced the number of seminaries by one. New statements on "The Ministry of all Christians," the creation of a new "Diaconal Ministry" for full-time lay professionals and an improved candidacy plan for ordinands resulted. The perennial question about whether district superintendents should be elected or appointed was resolved in favor of the appointed pattern. Life tenure for bishops was reviewed. Some argued that "term" episcopacy, which was the Evangelical United Brethren pattern, would encourage the election of bishops who would be relatively young or female or of ethnic minority background. Others argued that limiting the term of bishops would only increase the power of church agency executives. Life tenure for bishops won, but their service as episcopal leaders in one geographical area was cut to a maximum of eight years.

Both the Methodist and Evangelical United Brethren churches came to union in 1968 with strong statements on social principles that guided their life and witness. The new church ended up with not one but two statements of social principles—an aging Methodist Social Creed, originally adopted in 1908, and the Evangelical United Brethren "Basic Beliefs Regarding Social Issues and Moral Standards." Similar at some points, they were sufficiently different at others to raise penetrating questions about their theological and ethical foundations. Furthermore, the new church faced a new world situation; old problems were becoming more complex and difficult new ones had arisen. A quadrennial study commission was appointed by the uniting conference to resolve the matter. In the end a fresh new statement of social principles, plus a new social creed for use in services of worship, was adopted.

The new statement began with a call to responsible use of this world's natural resources. It gave vigorous support for birth control and limitation of population growth, as well as cautious approval to abortion and remarriage of divorced persons. The right of responsible civil disobedience was recognized; support for conscientious objectors was extended to include opposition to particular wars. More explicit approval was given to the struggle for racial and social justice. The statement on human sexuality was the most difficult of all to resolve. The study commission followed arguments from legal and medical professionals by recognizing homosexuals as "persons of sacred worth who need the ministry and guidance of the church" and whose "human and civil rights need to be ensured." But the conference voted with the people back home in affirming that the church does "not condone the practice of homosexuality" and considers it "incompatible with Christian teaching."

The Flowering of Caucus Methodism

When United Methodists gathered for their first General Conference in 1972, they found themselves struggling to understand what it means to be a pluralistic as well as a united church. The large number of persons wearing badges and buttons, handing out newsletters, holding press conferences, buttonholing delegates, startled many. The event marked the coming age of United Methodism's growing family of caucuses — the ethnic caucuses (Asians, blacks, Hispanics, and Native Americans) along with women, youth, seminarians, and gays. The sixty-year-old Methodist Federation for Social Action on the left had been joined by the youthful Good News Movement on the right. The time had come, each said in its own way, to redress the balance and rediscover the rich diversity of the Methodist family.

American society had undergone tremendous cultural and social transformation in the 1960s. The rise of ethnic minority feeling indicated a renewed search for identity as well as a search for power. The United Methodist Church, which has the largest ethnic constituency of any American church, was being challenged to affirm the cultural differences of its ethnic representatives and allow them to express their faith in terms of their own life-style and cultural heritage.

The uniting conference of 1968 established a Commission on Religion and Race to promote the church's goal of developing a racially inclusive church. The 1972 General Conference made it a permanent commission with an expanded mandate. Since ethnic churches represent the area of highest potential for church growth or loss, the 1976 and 1980 General Conferences named the Ethnic Minority Local Church as one of the church's highest priorities.

Black Methodists for Church Renewal (BMCR), a national forum for black United Methodists, was formed in the midst of the civil rights movement of the 1960s. Formally organized in 1968, the caucus avoided the call of militant leaders inside the church and out to separate from the white church and early announced its intention to work for change from within. By 1970 chapters were formed in all the jurisdictions and many of the annual conferences, and a monthly tabloid called NOW was being widely circulated. Over the next few years BMCR chalked up an impressive record of achievements. It lobbied for the Commission on Religion and Race, urged church agencies to upgrade the level of black leadership, and secured a General Conference commitment to raise substantial funds for the church's black colleges and their students. By the early 1970s, however, BMCR had to share the minority spotlight with other groups.

United Methodism's most rapidly growing ethnic minority group is its Asian-American community. Early in this century, Chinese, Japanese, Korean, and Filipino Methodist churches had been organized into separate mission annual conferences. In the postwar years it was felt that Methodists of all ethnic and national backgrounds should be united into one fellowship. Thus the Oriental Mission Conference, including Chinese, Korean, and Filipino churches, was dissolved in 1952. The Japanese mission conference survived the terrible years of "relocation" during World War II and continued until 1964 when it merged with the California-Nevada Annual Conference. In recent years, however, many Japanese-American United Methodists began to regret the loss of their identity and, together with Chinese, Korean, and Pacific Islanders, organized a National Federation of Asian American United Methodists to map strategy. A decisive early victory was the election of Wilbur Choy as bishop in 1972. More recently, the caucus has issued a new call for the formation of an Asian American mission conference.

*T*hrough the years many United Methodists have felt that Edwin Markham's words about a circle being drawn that shut certain persons out applied to them—women, blacks, youth, Hispanics, persons with handicapping conditions, Native Americans, children, Asian Americans, and others. Recently the excluded persons have taken the lead in enlarging the circle to take all persons in and give them places of responsibility in The United Methodist Church.

We drew a circle that shut them out...

But Love and I had the wit to win: We drew a circle that took them in

Native American United Methodists, though scattered in small numbers around the country, are largely concentrated in Oklahoma where they have been organized as an Indian mission conference since 1844. Now twelve thousand strong they are led by seventy ministers and four district superintendents, all of whom are Native American. The current revival of Indian culture led to the formation in 1970 of the Native American International Caucus (NAIC). Support for voting rights at jurisdictional and general conferences, efforts to raise education standards and salaries of pastors, and communication among the fifty widely scattered churches outside the Oklahoma area have been NAIC's persistent concerns.

Treated for decades as a stepchild of home missions activity, the Hispanic churches in Texas, with the formation of the Methodist Church in 1939, achieved status as a separate Rio Grande Annual Conference, which spreads over the lower Rio Grande River valley with headquarters in the heavily Spanish flavored city of San Antonio. The development of Hispanic-American Methodism in the large cities on both coasts, as well as in the Southwest, runs counter to the tendency of other European ethnic ministries to merge with predominantly English-speaking conferences. A strong intention to maintain this visible distinction from the "Anglo" churches of the region is evident from the leadership of the national Hispanic caucus, Methodists Associated Representing the Cause of Hispanic Americans (MARCHA), formed in 1971. High on MARCHA's agenda is the election of an Hispanic bishop.

The Commission on the Status and Role of Women (CSRW), created in 1970 and fully funded in 1972, was a second crucial new churchwide commission. Together with the United Methodist Women's Caucus, it has kept women's concerns on the agendas of conferences and councils across the church. Women no longer seeking careers in

Christian education or mission but in the ordained ministry, began to enter seminaries in increasing numbers. By 1980 women represented more than 3 percent of the total professional ministry, an increase of 75 percent over 1975. While some local churches resist the idea of a woman pastor, the appointment system does assure women of employment in ministry. A few women have been appointed district superintendent beginning with Margaret Henrichsen in Maine in 1967; the number grew to seven by 1980. A major breakthrough occurred that year when Marjorie Matthews was elected bishop.

Modern Methodism's oldest caucus, the Methodist Federation for Social Action (MFSA), highly suspect during the "red scare" of the 1950s, found new life and a new focus in the civil rights and antiwar movements of the 1960s. Led by an energetic executive secretary, new annual conference chapters were formed and circulation of its *Social Questions Bulletin* doubled. The MFSA's long-standing critique of capitalism and support for organized labor were now coupled with liberation theology and promotion of J. P. Stevens and Nestle boycotts.

Highly visible and institutionally successful among the caucuses is the Good News Movement, which identifies itself as a "Forum for Scriptural Christianity Within the United Methodist Church." Founded in 1966, Good News publishes a popular monthly journal, along with newsletters for women and seminarians, and information sheets on such issues as missions, church school curriculum, and legislative strategy. It sponsors large-group convocations and small-group "think tank" meetings, "renewal groups" in the annual conferences, and has a major program aimed at making mission programs more evangelical. The caucus, which has already produced confirmation literature of its own, has called on those responsible for church school curriculum to produce a track of distinctively evangelical literature.

A cluster of newer caucuses has emerged more recently. The Coalition for the Whole Gospel, formed early in 1979, aims to provide a counter force to Good News by fostering unity among the other caucuses on common issues. United Methodist Renewal Services Fellowship, a charismatic group formed as an outgrowth of the interdenominational Conference on Charismatic Renewal held during the summer of 1977, publishes a monthly newsletter MANNA and holds national conferences to nourish spirit-filled United Methodists. There is also an organized fellowship of gay United Methodists. Some one hundred persons, gay and straight, met in November 1978 in New York City at an "Education Conference on Homosexuality and The United Methodist Church." The constitution of the group was changed to allow the election of a female along with a male to head the organization and a new name was adopted: Affirmation. A principal goal of Affirmation is full laity and clergy rights for gay persons in The United Methodist Church.

Theological and Liturgical Renewal

The doctrinal consensus of which Methodists, Evangelicals, and United Brethren boasted in the nineteenth century was badly shattered by twentieth-century theological fads. The result was a loosening of ties to the churches' theological traditions. In the post–World War II period a few zealous Methodists, Evangelicals, and United Brethren tried to hold the old lines of Fundamentalism or Liberalism. More and more, however, equally zealous persons came forward to advocate the new theological fashions as they came along.

The churches' soaring optimism was severely tested by the successive tragedies of two world wars, the great depression in between, and the rise of communism, fascism, and Nazism. The liberal dream of a world becoming progressively better persisted, but the dreamers grew more anxious and less certain in the face of repeated disenchantments. This set the stage for a rebirth of interest in the One who stands above the tangle of human affairs. Divine initiative, human sin, revelation through Christ, and salvation by faith were newly fashionable under the label of "Neo-Orthodoxy." It was a great epoch in theology, but its direct impact on the churches was negligible.

In the 1950s Christian existentialism, which stressed faith as a vivid personal experience, appealed to evangelicals who wanted to be modern. At the same time, a small cadre of Methodists was rediscovering Wesley, and the ecumenical movement was leading others to reconsider basic doctrines of church, ministry, and the sacraments.

The flare of hope aroused by the election of John F. Kennedy in 1960 called forth more radical theological options. The "death of God" hurrah and the flurry about the "Secular City" emerged and found their share of followers. A new interest in Oriental faiths led others to become devotees of Zen Buddhism and followers of itinerant Hindu gurus. By the 1970s, while evangelicals were reawakening and charismatics were feeling the spirit, liberation theologies began to take center stage—black theology, feminist theology, third-world theology.

The constitution of The United Methodist Church, following the Methodist pattern, explicitly prohibits any alterations in "our present, existing and established standards of doctrine." The new *Book of Discipline* was full of procedures by which clergy and laity could be censured for teachings contrary to these doctrines. Yet nowhere were "our doctrines" defined and scarcely anywhere were they understood. The joint committee on church union simply printed back to back in the new Discipline the Methodist Articles of Religion dating from 1784 and the recently updated Evangelical United Brethren Confession of Faith of 1962, and the Judicial Council deemed them "congruent, if not identical in their doctrinal perspective and not in conflict." Yet they were not identical and explicit references to the traditional Wesleyan foundations (Wesley's "standard" *Sermons* and *Notes Upon the New Testament*, for instance) were absent from the plan of union.

As a result of this confusion, the uniting conference established a Theological Study Commission on Doctrine and Doctrinal Standards. It was assumed that the commission would prepare a new creed to replace the historic statements inherited from the former Methodist and Evangelical United Brethren churches. Sensing that such a course was doomed to fail, the commission formulated a new setting into which the early faith statements were placed as foundation documents. Scripture, tradition, experience, and reason were all recognized as theological guidelines. Diversity among United Methodist views was acknowledged.

The commission's report was adopted by the General Conference in 1972. United Methodism refused to become a creedal church and instead continues to set scripture, tradition, experience, and reason in interaction with each other as resources for doing theology. The report envisions that church people will put theology on the agendas of all their conferences and councils, commissions and committees.

Liturgy

Two widely different styles dominated church architecture of the 1950s and 1960s — red-bricked, white-pillared, tall-spired colonial or clean-lined, natural finished, A-framed modern. Widely different styles of worship services were held in them. Major revisions of worship services occurred in 1959 when the Evangelical United Brethren Church revised its *Book of Ritual* and in 1964 when the Methodists revised their *Book of Worship* and *Book of Hymns*; all three are still in use. Sixteenth-century words and phrases dominate because the revisions were essentially a recovery of inherited liturgies. Published on the eve of a decade-long movement of liturgical renewal, both churches were unable to take full advantage of the new insights that soon brought forth fresh liturgies from sister churches, Catholic and Protestant alike. Mid-sixties worship leaders, refusing to believe that recovery of past forms was the answer to making worship authentic and relevant, preferred to experiment with new forms of worship. So casual communions and chummy prayers, balloons and banners, guitars and folksongs predominated.

To bring order out of chaos the newly united church in 1970 authorized an Alternate Rituals Project. The proposed 21-volume Supplemental Worship Resources series was by far the most ambitious worship project in history. The new liturgies and worship resources were not designed to replace the service books of 1959 and 1964, but to give United Methodists more options. The first in the series, a new Lord's Supper service, was published in English in 1972, in Spanish in 1978, and in Japanese in 1982. In contemporary language, the service is not simply a revision of Wesleyan texts, but an attempt to follow classical and universal patterns. Fresh services of baptism (with confirmation and renewal possibilities) followed in 1976 and new wedding and burial rites in 1979. Along the way United Methodists traded the literary preaching of the early decades of this century for preaching based on a set of scripture readings for each Sunday. Free-standing communion tables replaced altars attached to the chancel wall. White robes and colorful stoles replaced the long-standing ministerial black.

New Ecumenical Ventures

To the flowering of United Methodism's long standing caucus tradition and attempts at doctrinal and liturgical renewal, was added in the late 1960s and early 1970s, participation in new ecumenical ventures. The church took a giant step toward supporting Christian unity by adopting a major new resolution on "open" (versus closed or family) ecumenism in 1968. The resolution acknowledged the imperatives of the gospel toward unity and pledged United Methodism's continued participation in the ecumenical movement at all levels. Support for the National Council of Churches and World Council of Churches continued despite criticism of certain (mostly social) programs. Enthusiasm for the Consultation on Church Union, a continuing plan to unite the major American Protestant denominations, waned. However, something new appeared on the ecumenical horizon and United Methodists were eager to join.

Bilateral conversations with the Roman Catholics on a national and international level began in 1966. The purpose was to explore what is held in common and to consider honestly what the chief problems are that separate. The conversations, which led to the publication in 1976 of a progress report entitled "Growth in Understanding," included consensus statements on the Lord's Supper, ministry and authority in the two churches. Interreligious dialogue with Jews was begun in 1972 and with Islam in 1980; inter-Methodist dialogue with the three independent black Methodist churches was begun in 1979 and with other members of the Wesleyan family of American churches in 1980. In order to have a more effective ecumenical voice for and to the whole church, the 1980 General Conference created a separate General Commission on Christian Unity.

*A*lthough the Methodist Episcopal Church advertised its cooperation with the government's war effort in 1917, The United Methodist Church said in 1980 that "the production, possession, or use of nuclear weapons" must "be condemned."

Conclusion

by John G. McEllhenney

United Methodism's story has now been told, so it is time to consider what can be learned from this history with regard to the future. First, however, some comments on history itself are in order.

History offers us clues for solving the future's mystery. By knowing the past we can hazard guesses about the years ahead. Once we have studied the Bible and church history, we can form some notion of what to expect in United Methodism's future.

We learn from the Bible that God works in history through a combination of promises kept and surprises. This point is made in Isaiah 48, where God says two things that sound contradictory at first, but which, when held together, say all that can be said about the role of the past in understanding the present and predicting the future.

First, God says to the exiles in Babylon: "The former things I declared of old . . .; then suddenly I did them and they came to pass . . . I declared them to you from of old . . . lest you should say, 'My idol did them . . .'" (Isaiah 48:3-5). In this passage the people of Israel are reminded that God had revealed to them the divine plans so that when they came to pass they would give credit to God and not to their idols.

God speaks to us in similar fashion through history, say-ing: "Notice how I have interacted with human actions in the past and expect something like it to happen in the future. Do not be caught off guard. Learn from the past how to manage better in the future." On the one hand, God urges us to learn from history what to expect in the days ahead.

On the other hand, God says that history is full of surprises. In the discussion recorded in Isaiah 48, God goes on to say to the exiles: "I make you hear new things . . . They are created now, not long ago; before today you have never heard of them, lest you should say, 'Behold, I knew them.'" (48:6-7) Here God tells the people of Israel to be prepared for some surprises, some things that never happened before.

History, then, repeats certain patterns, but it does not clone itself. It does not make exact copies of past events. Always there is something new in the midst of the familiar. If we are to learn therefore from history about the weaving together of human and divine actions, we must learn to look for patterns that are likely to be repeated, while expecting the patterns to be varied in unexpected ways.

We can learn from United Methodist history to expect God to renew the church through efforts similar to John Wesley's attempts to renew the eighteenth-century Church of England. That church, following a century of conflict, was calm. During the previous century some Anglicans had led one side in the English Civil War; others had led the opposition. Their beliefs had become battle cries; their swords had been unsheathed in the name of differing views of the church. Once the war was over, they made up their minds to keep their church from being torn apart again.

A damper was placed on religious intensity. Believers were urged to be reasonable about their beliefs. The result was the Church of England known to Wesley, a church so moderate in its presentation of Christianity that many found it spiritually chilly.

Because Wesley's spirit shivered in the Church of England, he set out to warm it. Its leaders, however, looked at his renewal activities through lenses ground by seventeenth-century religious battles. Concluding that Wesley was undermining their church's hard-won moderation, they refused to cherish him as a God-sent harbinger of the Spirit, with the result that Methodism became a new church instead of being the bearer of renewal within the Church of England.

Today's United Methodist Church is the outcome of decisions not unlike those that produced Anglican moderation in the eighteenth century. Its component churches experienced the excitement of religious revivals and the divisiveness of the American Civil War in the nineteenth century. They tamed enthusiasm and overcame old estrangements in the twentieth century. Yet the organizational harmony of United Methodism has been purchased at a price: the loss of the crackling Christianity of Wesley, Otterbein, and Albright.

No official program will rekindle the fire, because new spiritual life always comes as a surprise. No Anglican bishop appointed Wesley to renew the Church of England; no Reformed synod commissioned Otterbein to renew the Reformed Church; no Lutheran pastor chose Albright to renew the Lutheran Church. Renewal came through individuals who had received from God a new key to human minds and hearts. Where they spoke people gathered. And having gathered once to hear a fresh word about God's love in Christ, they went on gathering for the purpose of growing in the Christian faith.

The challenge for the church within which such a renewal has begun is one of giving its leaders freedom to be themselves in God's service while holding them accountable to the fullness of the biblical revelation and the characteristics of a complete church. Unfortunately the Bible and church history offer few accounts of renewal leaders being given opportunities to bring new life to the institutions that nourished them. Jesus appeared as the Messiah in the midst of a community immersed in messianic expectations, but he was too much of a divine surprise for that community to welcome him.

On the basis of the preceding thoughts, what can we expect to happen in United Methodism's future? We can expect the church to be concerned for maintaining the characteristics of Christian completeness. Orders of worship, works of theological scholarship, ways of instructing laity and clergy, structures for involving laity and clergy in church government, benevolent institutions, the arts employed for the edification of believers and the glorification of God – all these are shown by history to be the way God's good news in Jesus Christ is kept intact and handed on from generation to generation.

But maintaining a complete church and guarding the fullness of the biblical revelation is not enough. As we saw in the Introduction, the Church of England in 1738 had the message people needed to hear, but that message was not being heard outside the walls of the church and scarcely within them. Then in May of that year God acted in and through John Wesley to do something new. Wesley got God's good news out to people by preaching in marketplaces and fields.

When we ponder the beginning of Wesley's work, we can imagine a student of the Bible and church history predicting in 1735 that the Church of England was ripe for a new burst of spiritual energy, but we cannot imagine anyone predicting that in May 1738 God would change a prissy spiritual introvert into a powerful extrovert for Christ. Yet God worked just such a transformation in Wesley.

As students of the Bible and United Methodist history, we can see that The United Methodist Church is ripe for a new burst of spiritual energy. We can expect on the basis of all that we know about the past that God will choose leaders able to help individuals find within the system of carefully thought out Christian beliefs a set of heartfelt personal convictions. We can also expect to be surprised by the leaders God will choose to be the obstetricians of a new spiritual birth.

Will we, however, be so surprised by the leaders that we will say what the people of Nazareth said about Jesus: "Where did this man get all this? What is the wisdom given to him? What mighty works are wrought by his hands! Is not this the carpenter, the son of Mary and brother of James and Joses and Judas and Simon, and are not his sisters here with us?" (Mark 6:2-3)

History does not tell us whether we will be so shocked by the obstetricians that our new spiritual birth will miscarry. The answer to that question falls into the category of God's new doings, things we have not heard about before, lest we should say, "Behold, I knew them." Therefore, we must move from history to hope—hope that God will open our minds and hearts to receive the men and women chosen by God to bring us renewal.

Bibliography

Ahlstrom, Sydney E., *A Religious History of the American People.* New York: Doubleday, 1975, 2 vols. Paperback.

Helps set United Methodist history in its larger American religious context.

Behney, J. Bruce and Paul H. Eller, *The History of the Evangelical United Brethren Church.* Nashville: Abingdon Press, 1979.

The standard history of the Evangelicals and United Brethren from their beginnings through union with the Methodists in 1968.

Brauer, Jerald C., *Protestantism in America: A Narrative History.* Revised edition. Philadelphia: Westminster Press, 1972. Paperback.

Places United Methodist history in the context of American Protestantism.

George, Carol V. R., *Segregated Sabbaths.* New York: Oxford University Press, 1973. Paperback.

The story of American Methodism's mission to blacks and the formation of independent congregations and national churches to 1840.

Langford, Thomas A., *Practical Divinity: Theology in the Wesleyan Tradition.* Nashville: Abingdon, 1983. Paperback.

Traces the development of Methodist theology from Wesley to the middle of the 20th century.

Norwood, Frederick A., *The Story of American Methodism*. Nashville: Abingdon Press, 1974. Paperback.
The basic survey.

Outler, Albert C., ed. *John Wesley*. New York: Oxford University Press, 1964. Paperback.
Judicious selections from Wesley's writings, plus helpful introductions and commentary.

Thomas, Hilah F. and Rosemary Skinner Keller, *Women in New Worlds: Historical Perspectives on the Wesleyan Tradition*. Nashville: Abingdon, 1981-2. 2 vols. Paperback.
Lively essays on various contexts in which United Methodist women have exercised their ministry: home and family, laity and clergy roles in the churches, leadership in reform movements in society.

For Further Information
United Methodist Studies: Basic Bibliographies, compiled by Kenneth E. Rowe. Nashville: Abingdon, 1982. Paperback.

Index

A

Affirmation, 122
African Methodist Episcopal Church, 40, 75
African Methodist Episcopal Zion Church, 40, 75
Albright, Jacob, 2, 9, 33, 34, 35, 44, 51, 87, 94, 100, 131
Albright's People, 34
Alcohol, beverage (characteristic #5), 30, 37, 51, 53, 56, 84, 86, 96
Allen, Richard, 31, 40, 42
Andrew, James O., 66, 67
Architecture, church (characteristic #6), 3, 15, 38f, 56, 77, 93, 100f, 124f, 132
Asbury, Francis, 19, 21, 23, 24, 26, 27, 28, 31, 35, 37, 38, 39, 40, 44, 49, 50, 87

B

Bangs, Nathan, 60
Baxter, John, 31
Becker, Samuel, 34
Benevolent Institutions (characteristic #5), 3, 5, 51, 132

Black Methodists for Church Renewal, 117f
Black, William, 30
Boardman, Richard, 18, 19, 21
Boehm, Martin, 9, 13, 14f, 24, 36, 44, 87

C

Camp Meetings (characteristic #1), 44, 50, 55, 56, 78
Caucuses (characteristic #3), 117-122, 125
Choy, Wilbur, 118
Christian Methodist Episcopal Church, 75
Christmas Conference, 28-31, 53
Church and Society (characteristics #2 and #5), 3, 37, 51, 53, 63, 70, 84f, 114, 116
Church, characteristics of a complete, 2f, 4, 5, 131, 132
Church of England (Anglican Church), 1, 2, 4, 9, 11, 18, 26, 27, 36, 96f, 130, 131, 132
Church of the Nazarene, 78

Clergy *(characteristic #4)*, 2, 3, 5,
 21, 24f, 26f, 28, 30, 34, 36,
 38, 39f, 42, 43, 51, 52f,
 53f, 55, 56, 58f, 61f, 66,
 68f, 71, 76, 77, 79, 80f,
 93, 98f, 101, 104, 111,
 114, 115, 121, 122, 123,
 125, 126, 132
Coalition for the Whole
 Gospel, 122
Coke, Thomas, 26, 27, 30,
 31, 37, 38, 43
Coker, Daniel, 40
Colleges *(characteristic #5)*, 3, 30,
 38, 58, 76, 118
Colored Methodist Episcopal
 Church, 75
Commission on Religion and
 Race, 117, 118
Commission on the Status and
 Role of Women, 120
Conscientious objection to war
 (characteristic #5), 23, 108,
 113f, 116, 121
Consultation on Church
 Union, 112, 126
Cope, Catherine, 33
Creighton, Thomas, 26f
Cromwell, James, 30

D

Darwin, Charles, 74, 78
Dempster, James, 23
Dickins, John, 38, 40
Doctrine *(characteristic #2)*, 3, 5,
 11, 18f, 27, 28, 34, 37, 42,
 43, 50, 58, 60f, 77ff, 99ff,
 102, 114, 116, 121, 122ff,
 125f, 130, 132f
Dreisbach, John, 35, 38
Dress, 22, 38, 53, 56, 77, 125

E

Ecumenical Methodist
 Conferences, 87, 111
Ecumenical Movement, 87, 102,
 111f, 125f
Education *(characteristic #4)*, 3, 5,
 38, 55, 56-59, 67, 68f, 74,
 76
Edwards, Jonathan, 10
Embury, Philip, 15, 16, 31
Ethnic Minority Local Church
 Priority, 117
Ethnic Minorities
 Asians, 83, 98, 117, 118
 Blacks, 31, 40f, 60, 74f, 76,
  100, 101, 102-105, 109ff, 117f
 Hispanics, 83, 98, 117, 120
 Immigrants, 83, 97f
 Native Americans, 9, 10, 43,
  60, 82, 83, 117, 120
 Representation *(characteristic #3)*,
  115, 117
EVANGELICAL MOVEMENT,
 3, 4, 37, 38, 97, 122
Evangelical Association, 33ff,
 39, 42f, 45, 50, 51f, 52, 53,
 54f, 58, 59, 61, 63f, 75, 78,
 79, 82, 83, 84, 86, 93, 94f,
 97, 98, 99, 100, 101
Evangelical Church, 99, 102,
 107, 108, 109, 111
EVANGELICAL UNITED
 BRETHREN CHURCH,
 107, 109, 110, 111, 112,
 113, 115, 116, 123, 124

F

Federal Council of
 Churches, 86, 87, 102
Fundamentalism *(characteristic #2)*,
 99, 122

G

Garrettson, Freeborn, 27, 30
Garrison, William Lloyd, 63
Geeting, George Adam, 36
Good News Movement, 117, 121
Government, church (*characteristic #3*), 3, 5, 28-31, 34f, 36f, 38, 39f, 42f, 53ff, 61f, 65ff, 67f, 68f, 74f, 77ff, 79ff, 96f, 98f, 101-105, 109ff, 112, 113, 114ff, 117-122, 123, 131ff
Great Awakening, 10, 12
Grosh, Christopher, 36

H

Hammett, William, 39
Harding, Francis, 66
Heck, Paul and Barbara, 16
Henrichsen, Margaret, 121
Historic Churches
    African Zoar, 40
    Barratt's Chapel, 27
    John Street, 16
    Lovely Lane, 28
    Mother Bethel, 40
    St. George's, 18, 19, 21, 31, 38, 40
History, 129f, 132f
Hoffman, Joseph, 36
Holiness Movement, 77f
Homosexuality, 116, 117, 122
Hopkey, Sophey, 10
Hosier, Harry, 31
Houtz, Anthony, 33

J

Jackson, Andrew, 61
Johnson, Lyndon B., 113
Johnson, Samuel, 1f, 23

K

Kemp, Frederick, 36
Kennedy, John F., 123
King, Lord Peter, 26

L

Laity, 2, 11, 15f, 38, 52, 53, 58, 61f, 68, 70, 76, 77, 79f, 98, 123, 132
Lambert, Jeremiah, 31
Lee, Robert E., 70
Liberalism (*characteristic #2*), 78, 99f, 122
Lincoln, Abraham, 70
Liesser, Samuel, 34
Long, Isaac, 14
Lutheran Church, 2, 4, 9, 33, 34, 97, 131

M

Matthews, Marjorie, 121
McGee, John and William, 44
McKendree, William, 44
McNamar, John, 54
Mennonites, 9, 14
METHODIST MOVEMENT, 1, 3, 4, 9-12, 13, 15-20, 21-28, 37, 53, 60, 77f, 83, 84, 93, 94f, 96f, 99, 100, 122, 123
Methodist Episcopal Church in America, 28-31, 34, 35, 36, 38, 39-42, 42f, 44f, 50, 51, 52, 53, 55, 56, 58, 59, 60, 64-70, 70f, 74, 75, 76, 77, 79f, 82f, 86, 87, 98f, 100, 101, 102ff
Methodist Protestant Church, 61f, 64, 75, 76, 79, 80, 82f, 86, 98, 100, 104, 111

Methodist Episcopal Church, South, 67-70, 70f, 74f, 75, 76, 77, 79, 82f, 86, 87, 98, 99, 100, 101, 102ff
Methodist Church, The, 105, 107, 108, 109, 110, 111, 112, 113, 115, 116, 124
Methodist Federation for Social Service/Action, 86, 117, 121
Methodists Associated Representing the Cause of Hispanic Americans, 120
Miles, William H., 75
Miller, George, 34f
Miller, Solomon, 35
Missions (characteristic #5), 3, 9, 55, 59f, 67, 74, 80, 82f, 97, 102, 121
Moody, Dwight L., 84
Moravians, 10f
Mott, John R., 111
Mueller, Reuben H., 113

N

Nast, William, 83
National Council of Churches, 126
National Federation of Asian American United Methodists, 118
Native American International Caucus, 120
Newcomer, Christian, 36
Newly Formed Methodist Connection, 34
Nixon, Richard M., 114

O

O'Kelly, James, 26, 39f
Opheral, Charity, 80

Otterbein, Philip William, 2, 9, 13f, 24, 28, 36, 44, 51, 87, 100, 131
Oxnam, G. Bromley, 109

P

Parlin, Charles C., 108
Peace (characteristic #5), 94f, 107ff
Pilgrim Holiness Church, 78
Pilmore, Joseph, 18ff, 21, 31, 38
Pluralism, 117, 124
Primitive Methodist Church, 39
Publishing (characteristic #5), 3, 22, 35, 38, 43, 52, 55, 56, 60f, 66, 67, 68, 74, 75f, 97, 99

R

Racism, 102, 109ff, 117f
Rankin, Thomas, 21, 24
Reformed Church, 2, 4, 9, 13, 33, 34, 36, 97, 131
Renewal, 4f, 11, 130-133
Republican Methodist Church, 39
Revivalism (characteristic #1), 44, 50f, 56, 84, 131
Riegel, Adam, 33
Ryland, William, 36

S

Sacraments (characteristic #1), 2, 5, 11, 21, 24f, 27, 28, 53, 55f, 77, 86, 96, 123, 125, 126
Schisms, 39-42, 61f, 65-70, 77f, 86, 101f, 131
Scott, Orange, 65
Second Great Awakening, 50f, 63
Seminaries (characteristic #4), 59, 70, 76, 93, 99, 101, 115, 121

Sexism, 111
Sexton, Lydia, 80
Shadford, George, 21
Shaffer, Frederick, 36
Shaw, Anna Howard, 80
Slavery (characteristic #5), 30, 37,
    51, 63-67, 70, 87
Smith, Al, 96
Social Gospel (characteristic #2),
    84, 86
Soule, Joshua, 60, 67
Spencer, Peter, 42
Stewart, John, 43
Strawbridge, Robert, 15f, 18, 21
Sunday schools (characteristic #4),
    3, 55, 56f, 60, 76, 96,
    99, 121

T

Taylor, Thomas, 18
Thorne, Mary, 38
Tittle, Ernest F., 108

U

Union/Reunion discussions, 35,
    43, 74, 86f, 101-105, 107,
    112, 113, 114, 124
Union Church of Africans, 40f
UNITED BRETHREN
    MOVEMENT, 3, 4, 13ff,
    22, 28, 33, 37, 38
United Brethren in Christ,
    Church of, 35, 36f, 39, 42f,
    45, 50, 51, 52, 53, 54, 56,
    58, 59, 61, 63f, 75, 76, 78,
    79, 80, 82, 83, 84, 87, 93,
    94f, 97, 98, 99, 100, 101,
    107, 108, 109, 111, 122
United Brethren in Christ (Old
    Constitution), 78

United Evangelical Church, 78
UNITED METHODISM, 1, 2,
    3, 5, 9, 51, 75, 84, 87,
    97, 129-133
United Methodist Church, The,
    110, 112, 113-126
United Methodist Renewal
    Services Fellowship, 122
United Nations, 109

V

Vanderhorst, Richard H., 75
Vasey, Thomas, 27

W

Wars
    Civil, 70f
    Revolutionary, 23f, 37
    Vietnamese, 113f
    World War I, 93f
    World War II, 107ff
Washington, George, 37
Waugh, Beverly, 60
Webb, Thomas, 15, 16, 18
Wesley, Charles, 9, 10f
Wesley, John, 1f, 9-12, 13, 14,
    15, 16, 18, 19, 20, 21, 22,
    23, 26f, 28, 30, 35, 36, 37,
    38, 51, 60, 64f, 70, 77,
    100, 123, 124, 130ff
Wesleyan Methodist Church, 65
Whatcoat, Richard, 27, 44
White, Thomas, 23
Whitefield, George, 10, 11f, 13,
    15, 16
Wicke, Lloyd C., 113
Willard, Frances E., 79, 84
Williams, Robert, 21
Women, 38, 51, 79ff, 82f, 84,
    98f, 111, 115, 117, 120f

World Council of Churches, 111,
        126
World Methodist Council, 112
Worship *(characteristic #1)*, 2, 3,
        5, 22, 28f, 53, 55f, 77,
        100f, 102, 116, 124f, 132
Wright, Richard, 19

Y

Youth, 115, 117

This book has been designed with the same personal craftsmanship and concern for the reader as shown in the writing and editing. Our aim is to make this book attractive and readable, so that it will better serve the readers' needs, the authors' dreams, and provide hours of valuable pleasure.

Design concepts are by Blair Simon. Drawings are by Ann Simon. The text typeface is 12 point Janson. Titles and headlines are in Caslon Headline.

The preparation and typography were made at Simon Communications in Ardmore, Pennsylvania. Printing and cover design are by The United Methodist Publishing House in Nashville, Tennessee.